SOCIAL
WORK
SUPERVISION

Sage Sourcebooks for the Human Services Series

Series Editors: Armand Lauffer and Charles Garvin

Recent Volumes in This Series

SOCIAL WORK SUPERVISION
Contexts and Concepts

Ming-sum Tsui

Sage Sourcebooks for

the Human Services

SAGE Publications
Thousand Oaks ■ London ■ New Delhi

For information:

Sage Publications, Inc.
2455 Teller Road
Thousand Oaks, California 91320
E-mail: order@sagepub.com

Sage Publications Ltd.
1 Oliver's Yard
55 City Road
London EC1Y 1SP
United Kingdom

Sage Publications India Pvt. Ltd.
B-42, Panchsheel Enclave
Post Box 4109
New Delhi 110 017 India

Printed in the United States of America

Library of Congress Cataloging-in-Publication data

Tsui, Ming-Sum.
Social work supervision: contexts and concepts / Ming-Sum Tsui.
        p. cm.
Includes bibliographical references and index.
ISBN 0-7619-1766-7 (cloth)—ISBN 0-7619-1767-5 (pbk.)
    1. Social workers—Supervision of. I. Title.
HV40.54.T78 2005
361.3′068′3—dc22

                                        2004005707

04   05   06   07   08   10   9   8   7   6   5   4   3   2   1

Acquiring Editor:	Arthur T. Pomponio
Editorial Assistant:	Veronica Novak
Production Editor:	Sanford Robinson
Typesetter:	C&M Digitals (P) Ltd.
Copy Editor:	Fran Anderson
Indexer:	Karen McKenzie
Cover Designer:	Glenn Vogel

Contents

Series Editor's Foreword

Professor Tsui in this book makes a substantial contribution to the contemporary literature on social work supervision. This literature, if it is to meet the reader's legitimate expectations, must have several aspects and all of these are addressed by this author. The first is that an understanding of supervision should be grounded in sound theoretical models. As is true of all of social work today, however, there are competing models such as those drawn from structural and organizational approaches and from practice theories themselves such as those based in one-on-one, group, and team dynamics. It is a sign of the strength of this book that the author can draw upon these various threads and create a sense of the complexity and yet wholeness of the supervisory process.

A second aspect of the social work scene today is a strong appreciation that any form of practice, including supervision, should draw from and contribute to empirical findings. Professor Tsui carefully examines research studies on supervision and relates these studies to theory building and to the practice of supervision. He identifies deficits in the empirical literature and proposes a future research agenda on supervision.

A third aspect is that there are many groups that have a stake in the outcomes of supervision such as the professional community, the agency, the practitioners, and the consumers of services. Tsui recognizes the legitimacy of all of these groups and indicates how the practice of supervision should relate to the needs of each of these groups, even when this may create dilemmas for the supervisor based on the demands placed by these diverse groups.

A fourth aspect is that a useful text on supervision must provide sufficient detail about practice to guide the activities of the supervisor. This book provides this amply through a discussion of the stages of supervision, the various functions a supervisor must fulfill, and the nature of the supervisory relationship.

All of the material in this book relates to several issues that must be strongly emphasized by all social workers. One is the inescapable fact that supervision, as well as all other social work activities, takes place in a world that is highly diverse in terms of ethnicity, culture, social class, and the intersection of these with gender dynamics. These forces are as influential in supervisory practice as in any other practice modality. Tsui, with the perspective that comes from his location in Asia as well as his education in the United States, offers unique insights into the role played by diversity in supervisory activities. Another issue, well understood by this author, is the importance of an understanding of power, especially when this is related to the similarities and differences between supervisors and supervisees.

I trust that you, the reader, will come away from this book with the sense that Professor Tsui's understanding of these topics has substantially enriched you in the ways that you will practice, either as supervisor or as supervisee and enable you, in turn, to make your own input into the field of social work supervision.

Charles Garvin

Preface

Social work supervision has been identified as one of the most important factors in determining the job satisfaction levels of social workers and the quality of service to clients. As an indirect, but vital, enabling social work process, it is surprising that supervision has not received as much attention as other components of social work practice, for example, social work research or social work administration. There is a noticeable lack of critical and in-depth discussion on the state of the art and evidence-based practice of social work supervision in the existing empirical research literature (Harkness, 1995; Tsui, 1997b, 2004). A review of the literature found that there is little theory or model building, and very few attempts to place supervisory practice within an organizational setting in a greater cultural context (Tsui & Ho, 1997).

It is clear, therefore, that a book on social work supervision is needed to bridge the gap between the demands of the field and the absence of literature. It should contain a description of the theoretical basis of supervision, a discussion of practice issues, and a consideration of the research implications. This is why *Social Work Supervision: Contexts and Concepts* was written. It is not only about what social work supervision should be but also about what it, in fact, is, and what it will be. It provides social work students with a basic knowledge of the theory and practice of supervision for social workers. It also facilitates class teaching by providing a general picture of the current state of the art of supervision for social work students. Teachers can then spend more time discussing specific supervisory issues and skills with their students. As one of the Sage Sourcebooks for the Human Services, this book is also intended to be a useful sourcebook for supervisors and frontline practitioners in the social work field.

This is a book on supervision for social workers. Its focus is not the fieldwork supervision of social work students in their practicum, although some of the major principles can be applied in this area. Still, staff supervision differs greatly from student supervision as it involves complicated organizational dynamics, hierarchies of administrative authority, and multiple accountabilities to various parties inside and outside a human service organization.

In this book, I present social work supervision as a rational, affective, and interactive process focusing on the whole person of the social worker. The focus should be generic and cover the values, knowledge, skills, and emotions of the staff. I perceive and, therefore, present supervision as a dynamic, multiparty, and interactional relationship within a specific organizational setting in a greater cultural context. These unique features differentiate social work supervision from "supervision" in the business sector, which focuses on human resource development and job monitoring, and from clinical supervision or psychotherapy supervision, which focuses on teaching clinical skills to therapists. Of course, knowledge and skills from business and psychotherapy contribute to a greater understanding of social work supervision—especially its educational functions.

The appearance of books on social work supervision has lagged far behind that of books on social work practice. The first reference on social work supervision, Virginia Robinson's (1936) *Supervision in Social Case Work*, was published nearly two decades after Mary Richmond's (1917) *Social Diagnosis*. In the first edition of his famous work, *Supervision in Social Work*, Kadushin (1976) outlined the three functions of social work supervision. In the third edition, Kadushin (1992a) also identified 15 major reference books published on social work supervision in North America since 1975 (Abels, 1977; Austin, 1981; Bunker & Wijnberg, 1988; Holloway & Brager, 1989; Kadushin, 1976, 1985; Kaslow, 1972; Kaslow et al., 1977; Middleman & Rhodes, 1985; Munson, 1979d, 1983; Pettes, 1979; Powell, 1980; Shulman, 1982; Westheimer, 1977). In the early 1990s, three popular books on social work supervision were published: *Supervision in Social Work* by Kadushin (1992a), *Clinical Social Work Supervision* by Munson (1993), and *Interactional Supervision* by Shulman (1993). In the new century, Munson published the *Handbook of Clinical Social Work Supervision* (2002), the third edition of his 1993 work. At the same time, Kadushin published the fourth edition of *Supervision in Social Work* with Daniel Harkness (Kadushin & Harkness, 2002). There are a few new references to specific areas of supervision, including supervision in a residential setting (Brown & Bourne, 1996), supervision in turbulent times (Hughes & Pengelly, 1997), and the supervisory relationship

(Kaiser, 1997). This suggests that the social work profession still depends on well-established scholars to revise and refine the state of the art of social work supervision. Obviously, there is significant need for us to revisit the subject.

If we take a look at the content of the literature on social work supervision, we find that, after more than a century of supervisory practice, a number of controversial issues still dominate the field (Tsui, 1997a). High on the list of unresolved debates is the issue of interminable supervision versus autonomous practice (Epstein, 1973; Kadushin & Harkness, 2002; Munson, 2002; Rock, 1990; Tsui, 1997a, 1997b; Veeder, 1990): one group of scholars advocates lifelong supervision for social workers while another group insists that autonomous professional practice should be encouraged after several years of direct practice in the same service setting.

Another much-debated and as yet unresolved issue concerns the balance of administrative, educational, and supportive functions (Abroms, 1977; Erera & Lazar, 1994b; Harkness & Poertner, 1989; Kadushin & Harkness, 2002; Munson, 2002; Payne, 1994; Shulman, 1993; Tsui, 1997a, 1997b). Some scholars assert that the educational function should be separated from the administrative functions because it is so difficult for frontline social workers to tell their own practice errors to supervisors who are monitoring their job performance. They proposed the introduction of external experts as consultants to enhance the professional knowledge and skills of frontline social workers. Then administrative supervisors can focus their attention and efforts on job performance monitoring and quality assurance. However, another group of scholars argue that if administrative supervisors do not take up the educational function, there is a gap between the administrative demands of the managers and staff development activities. For the same reason, staff may seek support from external sources (for example, a counselor in an employee assistance program), but this may not resolve the stress coming from the intra-organizational dynamics. The most valuable emotional support comes from immediate supervisors because it includes the recognition of job achievement.

Empirical studies of social work supervision are particularly scarce. An examination of the research literature published from 1950 to 2002 reveals the existence of only 34 such studies (see the Appendix). Furthermore, as Harkness and Poertner (1989) have pointed out, none of the empirical literature on social work supervision published in this period relates to client outcomes, even though efficient and effective service is ranked as the ultimate objective of social work supervision (Kadushin & Harkness, 2002; Munson, 2002; Shulman, 1993).

The practice of supervision not only influences the quality of service received by the client but also plays a significant role in the professional development of social workers. It is clearly, therefore, a very important aspect of social work practice. The dearth of up-to-date and critical literature based on empirical work exposes a gap between practice and research into that practice. Social work supervision, then, is an important area for us to investigate and invest to improve professional knowledge and practice.

There are 10 chapters in this book. Chapter 1 discusses the history, definition, and objectives of social work supervision. Chapters 2 and 3 discuss the theoretical models of social work supervision. In Chapter 4, different contexts for supervision are interpreted and discussed. In Chapters 5 and 6, the major functions of social work supervision—administrative, educational, and supportive—are discussed. Chapter 7 explores the power issues between supervisors and supervisees, which include the use of authority and the games played by supervisors and supervisees. The stages, strategies, and skills of supervision are discussed in Chapter 8. Chapter 9 is related to direct practice in supervision—the specific format and structure of supervision sessions. Chapter 10 provides a summary of the existing state of research studies on supervision and a vision of its future.

This book addresses the needs of four groups of potential readers, namely, social work students, social work educators, frontline practitioners, and social work supervisors. Of course, others who are interested in these topics may find it useful as well. The book can be used as a text for courses on social work supervision in schools of social work, as it contains a literature review of historical developments, theories and models, and empirical research studies. I hope that students and teachers, as well as supervisees and supervisors, find the book enjoyable and helpful.

Finally, and most important, this is a book that arose from practice experience in supervision and a book intended to enhance supervisory practice. I hope that the "vision" in this book, though it may not be "super," will eventually help us to realize and revitalize our mission in social work, that is, to benefit our clients. After all, that is the ultimate goal of social work supervision and also the objective of this book.

Acknowledgments

I am indebted to many people, including my teachers, supervisors, colleagues, and friends, who helped me to shape and sharpen my understanding of social work supervision. In addition, I wish to thank the graduate students in my classes on social work supervision, my fieldwork students over the past 20 years, and the participants in focus groups and in-depth interviews.

I give my warmest thanks to my teacher, Dr. Lynn McDonald, who insisted that I should focus my mind and my eyes on social work supervision. My sincere appreciation is also due to Dean Wes Shera, Dean Marion Bogo, Dr. Bernard H. K. Luk, and Dr. Gayla Rogers, who provided invaluable advice on my research.

Many thanks go to a number of widely published scholars: Dr. Pauline Erera, Dr. Bruce Thyer, Dr. Brij Mohan, Dr. Mike Austin, Dr. Alfred Kadushin, Dr. Daniel Harkness, Dr. Amnon Lazar, Mr. Kieran O'Donoghue, Dr. Carlton Munson, Dr. Lawrence Shulman, and Dr. Tamara Kaiser. I was lucky to have their encouragement and professional advice during the process of exploring the art of social work supervision. All I am trying to do is follow their path in the pursuit of knowledge and wisdom. Special thanks to Dr. Pauline Erera for her continuing encouragement; without her persistent support, this book would still be some rough ideas.

I cannot forget the unfailing support from my partners in conducting focus groups with supervisors and supervisees, Dr. Wui-shing Ho and Dr. Ching-man Lam, and my colleagues, Dr. Fernando C. H. Cheung and Dr. Charles Chan. All of them make me feel that I was not alone in the process of research, teaching, and writing.

Without the warm support and understanding of my wife, Doris, and my son, Lincoln, I could not have completed this book. In addition, my friends, Dr. C. Ruth Miller, Dr. Miu-chung Yan, Ms. Florence Lee, Dr. Matthew Peacock, and Miss Polly Chung, provided timely help and encouragement.

Finally, I must thank the Chief Editor of the Human Service Series, Dr. Charles Garvin, for his professional guidance during the writing process. In addition, Dr. Arthur Pomponio, Sanford Robinson, Paul Reis, Veronica Novak, Geri Mattson, Frances Andersen, Margaret Seawell, and Nancy Hale offered their professional support in an effective and efficient manner. I am happy to have had the opportunity to work with them. Their efforts made my dream come true and turned my ideas into a Sage book. In fact, this book is not so much a book of "mine," but a book of my "mind," nurtured by my dear family and friends.

1

The History, Definition, and Objectives of Social Work Supervision

The History of Social Work Supervision

Although the historical development of social work supervision provides critical insights into its nature, scant scholarly attention has been paid to this subject (Rabinowitz, 1987), and little effort has been made to search through the history of social work practice to discover when and how supervision arose. Only by tracing the roots of social work supervision can we understand its philosophy, identify its important and unique features, clarify its functions, and explain those functions in organizational and cultural contexts. As the history of social work supervision is lengthy (beginning in 1878), for the purpose of this review, it has been divided into five stages, each with its own dominant theme.

1. The Administrative Roots of Social Work Supervision

In North America, the roots of social work supervision can be found in the Charity Organization Societies (COS) movement, which began in 1878 in Buffalo, New York. Today, social work supervision has three main functions: administrative, educational, and supportive (Austin, 1957; Erera & Lazar, 1994a; Kadushin, 1976, 1985, 1992a; Kadushin & Harkness, 2002; Munson, 1979d, 1993; Payne, 1994; Poertner & Rapp, 1983; Shulman, 1993, 1995). There has been considerable debate as to which function was dominant during the early COS years. Some scholars suggest that supervision in social work was established to fulfill an educational function (*Encyclopedia of Social Work*, 1965; Kadushin, 1976, 1985, 1992a; Kadushin & Harkness, 2002), while others argue that social work supervision began as a form of administrative accountability (Austin, 1957; Kutzik, 1977; Waldfogel, 1983).

Those who believe education was the first function argue that educational supervision in the early COS years must have been necessary because most agency visitors were untrained volunteers (Kadushin & Harkness, 2002). However, Kutzik (1977) pointed out that, although untrained, the volunteer visitors came from the upper classes of society. In fact, they were board members of the agency, and they would not have been supervised by paid agents drawn from the middle and working classes who served as clerks or case assistants. As Kutzik (1977) observed, consultation rather than supervision was the rule among the COS settlement staff. The egalitarian nature of the COS movement made it difficult to establish the hierarchical relationship of administrative supervision. Hence, it can be concluded that there was an absence of administrative supervision in the early COS years (Kutzik, 1977). At the outset of the twentieth century, it became the practice to recruit agency visitors from the middle and working classes. There was a need to maintain a stable workforce of agency visitors. Some positions became paid jobs. Supervision then became a way for the top management of human service agencies to ensure administrative accountability. Given the historical context, it is likely that supervision was, at its inception, administrative rather than educational or supportive. Although many supervisors and frontline social workers think that the roots of social work supervision were educational or supportive, it is just the ideal, not the reality, of the history in the social work field.

Although the administrative function probably emerged first, educational and emotional support soon followed, during the early years of the twentieth century. As some agency visitors did not know how to offer help to the needy, there was a high turnover. Job orientation and training were carried out by the experienced and permanent agency staff (Kadushin, 1981; Kadushin & Harkness, 2002). However, the primary duties of the senior staff were still administrative, such as program planning, assigning workloads to the volunteers, and assessing the results of service delivery. At the same time, the supervisors also gave emotional support to agency visitors who felt frustrated in their work with clients. This is the earliest record of supportive supervision in the history of social work. Nevertheless, the dominant mode of supervision in the early years of the social work profession was administrative, and this continued to be the case throughout the twentieth century.

2. Change of Context: A Shift to the Educational Function

In 1898, a six-week summer training program was offered to 27 students by the New York Charity Organization Society. This was probably the first formal social work education program in the world. After several summer training programs, the New York School of Philanthropy was established in 1904; it offered a one-year program with student fieldwork instruction. It evolved into the first school of social work, which is now Columbia University's School of Social Work in New York City (Kadushin & Harkness, 2002; Rabinowitz, 1987).

In 1911, the first course in fieldwork supervision was offered under the sponsorship of the Charity Organization Department of the Russell Sage Foundation, headed by the highly respected social work pioneer, Mary Richmond (Kadushin, 1976, 1985, 1992a; Kadushin & Harkness, 2002). In the 1920s, the location for the training of social workers shifted from the human service agency to the university, and fieldwork supervision came to be viewed as an educational process that imparted the required values, professional knowledge, and practice skills to prospective social workers. Students learned social work practice at individual supervision sessions in their fieldwork placements (Munson, 2002). This format was derived from the tutorial system used in British universities such as Cambridge and Oxford. As a result of these educational roots, tutorials, and individual conferences were adopted as the most common formats for the supervision of social workers in human service agencies. According to Munson (2002), the form and structure of social work supervision have remained constant from the late nineteenth century to the present, but the content has evolved over the years. Social work supervision reflects the values of our society and the strategies of professional practice. It is natural that social work supervisors practice what they learned in college and adopt the role of tutor when they become social work supervisors. Thus, the individual conference has become the dominant format for social work supervision (Kadushin, 1992b; Ko, 1987). Student supervision, then, influences the format and content of staff supervision in the social work field, although the processes are different in terms of focus and structure (Bogo & Vayda, 1998). For some frontline social workers, student supervision remains the ideal format of social work supervision in the mind of frontline social workers (Tsui, 2001).

Prior to 1920, the social work literature contained no reference materials on social work supervision (Kadushin & Harkness, 2002). However, when fieldwork supervision became an integral part of social work education, it was no longer enough to teach "how" to be a social worker; a practice teacher had to be able to show students "why" social work strategies were effective, in order to make a training program competent and comprehensive. Student supervision was a mechanism for social work students to learn by doing. An experienced social worker oversaw the work of the student. Student supervision was seen as a key part of the learning process. Staff supervision and student supervision took separate paths, because the function of field instruction was primarily educational: it bridged the gap between the education provided by schools of social work and the reality encountered in human service organizations (Bogo & Vayda, 1987; Rogers & McDonald, 1992; Vayda & Bogo, 1991).

The teaching required some theoretical underpinnings. In 1936, Virginia Robinson published the first book on social work supervision, *Supervision in Social Case Work,* which defined supervision as "an educational process" (Robinson, 1936). Following her lead, there were 35 articles on supervision for caseworkers published between 1920 and 1945 in *The Family* (which was renamed *Social Casework* and is today *Families in Society*). During this period, the professional development of social workers became the primary purpose of social work supervision (Burns, 1958; Harkness & Poertner, 1989). For a long period of time, student supervision and staff supervision were considered similar. It was not until the mid-1960s that scholars and researchers began to recognize the conceptual, methodological, and practical differences between staff supervision and student supervision. Bogo and Vayda (1987) conceptualized the differences in terms of purpose and mission, activities, time perspective, primary focus, rewarded behaviors, approach, and method of governance.

According to Bogo and Vayda (1998), there are seven differences between the frame of reference of student fieldwork supervision and that of staff supervision. First, the purpose and mission of student fieldwork supervision is education, while that of staff supervision is quality of service to clients. Second, the core activities in a school of social work are teaching and research, while a human service organization emphasizes the effectiveness and efficiency of service delivery. Third, schools focus on future-oriented goals, for example, values orientation, knowledge education, and skill competence of the students, while social work agencies focus on present-oriented goals, that is, the provision of high-quality human services. Fourth, the primary focus of a school of social work is the analysis of current practice, while a human service organization focuses on the maintenance, enhancement, and effectiveness of current service programs. Fifth, the occupations of student fieldwork placement include critical analysis; developing, testing, and reporting new ideas; and independent intellectual activity. An organization pursues competent job performance, system maintenance, and inter-dependent teamwork. Sixth, the approach to social work in schools is rather general and abstract, but it is specific and concrete in the human service organization. Finally, the method of governance in schools is collegial and decisions are made by consensus, while a human service organization's authority is centralized and hierarchical, as it must be accountable to top management and funding bodies.

3. The Influence of Practice Theory and Methods

During the 1920s and 1930s, innovation in the field of social work was not limited to education. There were major changes in social work practice that had a profound impact on social work supervision. In the 1920s, psychoanalytic theory became an influential paradigm in the helping professions (Munson, 2002), which led to an integration of psychoanalysis and social work in the 1930s. Social workers borrowed selectively from psychoanalysis (and were especially drawn to the concept of the unconscious) to better understand the motivation, thoughts, feelings, and behaviors of both the social worker and the client. Social workers began to understand that self-awareness and understanding of their own personal attitudes and feelings are important to their professional practice. During this period, due to the pervasive influence of psychoanalytic theory, the supervisory process was viewed as a therapeutic process by social work supervisors

(Rabinowitz, 1987). Influenced by the psychoanalytic concepts of the unconscious, transference, and counter-transference, social workers became aware that their feelings, thoughts, and behaviors with clients were influenced by issues beyond their conscious awareness. To provide good service, the social worker must become "self-aware." The process of gaining self-awareness occurred during individual supervision sessions of analysis or therapy involving the supervisor and the supervisee. These sessions shed light on the personal and affective aspects of social work supervision.

Until the 1950s, the social casework method had a great impact on the format and structure of social work supervision (Austin, 1952; Munson, 2002; Towle, 1954). Some aspects of this method are still in evidence, such as the dyadic relationship between the supervisor and the supervisee and the confidentiality of the content of the supervisory session. Some supervisors even extend the concept of the "worker-client" supervisory model to include a "parallel process," which is called "isomorphism" in clinical supervision. It refers to a complex structure that is mapped onto another complex structure. This means the supervisees use the same skills to help their clients that their supervisors used to help them. Kahn (1979) noted that supervisors are aware of the workings of this parallel process. Both the treatment of clients and the supervision of staff require a good relationship between a more knowledgeable "expert" and a motivated learner. In both processes, cognitive and emotional capacities are engaged and an attempt is made to transfer "knowing" into "doing." However, the goals of treatment and supervision are different. For the client, the goal of social work intervention is personal growth, coping ability, and social functioning. For these purposes, the social worker makes a psychosocial diagnosis. For supervision, the major goal is to enhance professional growth in order for the supervisee to achieve a stable professional identity. What the supervisor does is to make an educational assessment and conduct staff development.

The casework approach to supervision, although still in use, has been rejected by many social workers who consider "caseworking the caseworker" a violation of the privacy of the supervisees (Kadushin, 1992b; Kadushin, & Harkness 2002; Ko, 1987; Munson, 2002). Helping professionals are also human beings whose privacy should be respected and protected. There are no grounds for the supervisor to examine the personal life of a supervisee unless the supervisee invites the supervisor to do so.

4. Debate Between Interminable
Supervision and Autonomous Practice

As we have seen, in the early years of social work practice, supervision was a means of monitoring the work of volunteers. At a later stage, formal social work training programs that included fieldwork supervision as part of the learning process were set up in universities. After the integration of psychoanalytic treatment theories and methods into social work practice, supervision became a therapeutic process for frontline social workers. By the 1950s, the therapeutic emphasis had waned and supervision came to be regarded as a stage in professional development for social workers (Rabinowitz, 1987). The psychodynamic influence remained in the supervisory process, but social work supervision evolved to become a lifelong process in the professional career of frontline social workers.

In the 1940s and 1950s, questions arose about the value of, and the need for, continuing social work supervision for professionally trained social workers (Austin, 1942; Bacock, 1953; Schour, 1951). With the creation of the National Association of Social Workers in the United States in 1956, social work took a significant step toward mature professionalization; however, the strong desire to achieve professional status soon led to a debate regarding professional autonomy. As independent practice and continual learning were regarded as two hallmarks of well-developed professions (Waldfogel, 1983), some social workers perceived extended supervision as an insult to their professional status and a symbol of their dependency, and began to search for alternatives (Austin, 1942; Eisenberg, 1956; Stiles, 1979). There was a movement away from "interminable" supervision toward autonomous practice, achieved after a number of years of professional practice (Austin, 1957; Munson, 2002). The advocates of autonomous practice maintain that a professional social worker with a master's in social work (MSW) and two to six years of experience in a specific service setting should be allowed to practice independently. He or she could consult an external expert whenever necessary.

The western New York chapter of the National Association of Social Workers (NASW) conducted the earliest empirical study of supervisory practice in 1958. Self-administered questionnaires were sent to all members ($N = 229$) of the western New York chapter. One hundred members returned completed questionnaires. The respondents generally felt satisfied with their supervision. However, they believed that there was a need to change supervision gradually in order to meet the needs of the individual staff. No respondent objected to supervisory authority or rejected the administrative functions of the supervisor; however, they considered the educational and supportive functions of supervision more useful.

5. A Return to the Administrative Roots in the Age of Accountability

As a result of the growth of managerialism that became prevalent in the 1980s, human service organizations have faced increasing demands from the government and the community to ensure that funding is spent in a "value-for-money" and "cost-effective" manner. Resources and funding are now dependent on the evaluation of the outcomes of service delivery. The quality of service is determined not only by professional practitioners but also by funding bodies and service consumers (Clarke, Gewirtz, & McLaughlin, 2000, 2001; Enteman, 1993; Flynn, 2000; Morgan & Payne, 2002; Pollitt, 1993; Tsui, 1998a; Tsui & Cheung, 2000b, 2004).

From the perspective of managerialism, the client is a customer, not a service consumer. The manager, not the frontline social worker, becomes the key person. Staff are viewed as employees, not as professionals. Management knowledge (not common sense or professional knowledge) is perceived as the core technology. The market, not society or the community, is the dominant environment. Cost effectiveness (that is, efficiency), not effectiveness, is the yardstick for organizational performance. Contracts replace care and concern as the bases of relationships. Under managerialism, the emphasis is on job performance, task orientation, standardization, documentation, consumerism, and cost awareness. The worker-client relationship becomes a transaction instead of a transformation (Tsui & Cheung, 2004). Influenced by all these changes, supervisors of human service organizations, and the profession as a whole, began, once again, to focus on the administrative function of supervision in order to promote effective and efficient service to clients.

This shift of focus is reflected in the changing definitions of social work supervision in five editions of the *Encyclopedia of Social Work*. In 1965, social work supervision was still defined as an educational process (*Encyclopedia of Social Work*, 1965); however, in the following three editions, the definitions were more administratively oriented

(*Encyclopedia of Social Work*, 1971, 1977, 1987). For example, the 1987 edition states that the new emphasis on the managerial functions of supervision reflects that an organic integration of the administrative and educational foci of supervision is crucial to enhancing the quality and productivity of human service organizations. In the 1995 edition, Shulman cited both the administrative and the educational functions. As he observed, "This emphasis on the educational aspect of supervision has over the years been combined with a second emphasis on administration that includes efforts to control and coordinate social workers to get the job done" (p. 2373). In the field of social work, the differentiation of supervision according to service settings has become apparent. For example, medical social workers have adopted a task-oriented approach to consultations with their supervisor due to the time-limited nature of cases in hospitals. Residential service and child welfare agencies focus on monitoring the performance of the frontline staff closely as is required by law. The nature of supervision has responded to changes in society and the task environment of specific types of human services.

THE DEVELOPMENT OF SOCIAL WORK SUPERVISION

In summary, social work supervision began as an administrative practice in the early Charity Organization Society years. At the beginning of the twentieth century, universities set up training programs, and gradually a body of knowledge and a theoretical framework for social work supervision emerged. Not surprisingly, supervision became an educational process. At the same time, the impact of psychoanalytic theory and its treatment methods led to the casework-oriented format and structure of supervision. When social work evolved into a mature profession, support grew for independent autonomous practice among social workers. However, due to the increasing demand for accountability in the past two decades, supervision has become administratively oriented again, in order to ensure quality of service to clients and the provision of resources for human service organizations.

The development of social work supervision can be perceived as the result of the influence of external funding bodies and the forces of professionalization over the past 125 years. Funding is influenced by many factors, including the prevalent socio-political views and the ideology of welfare. These forces determine the level of resources available for human service organizations and mold the administrative nature of social work supervision. The internal forces within the social work profession reflect the social workers' pursuit of respect and recognition for their professional status. They include the establishment of professional training institutes and professional associations, the use of scientific knowledge in practice, and the formulation of a code of ethics as a self-monitoring mechanism. At present, there is concern about the growth of private practices and developments in licensing legislation. The effect of these trends on social work supervision remains to be seen (Munson, 2002). It reflects that the development of social work supervision outlined previously is a historio-cultural process.

Munson (2002) observed that social work has made four major contributions to our society: (1) social reform; (2) client advocacy; (3) a short-term, cost-effective model of intervention; and (4) an effective model of supervision. This highlights the importance of social work supervision in social work's contribution to society. As social workers, we need to value our heritage. As supervisors, we need to pass on our experience and wisdom to the next generation. Social work practice is a continuing effort of human beings across generations to enhance the well-being of the people. In the same way, social work supervision should be perceived as a continual learning effort for both the supervisors and the frontline social workers to maintain the quality of service to their clients. Social work graduates often find that their training has not prepared them for the rapidly changing tasks of their work. Supervision is a bridge across the education-practice gap (Munson, 2002). In an era of accountability, social work supervision is sometimes viewed as merely a controlling mechanism that monitors frontline workers, but reduces their initiative and opportunities for creativity. This reduces the motives and space of creativity of the frontline social workers. As supervisors, we should not only instruct our staff but also inspire and impress them. The most important task of a supervisor is to convey the mission and vision with passion to supervisees. Then supervision becomes the shared mission of the older and younger generations of social workers. Social work supervision is not only a professional practice; it is also a moral practice.

As Munson (2002) observed, "Supervisors have a responsibility to know, understand, and convey to their supervisees a sense of the social work heritage. This heritage need not be conveyed in a technical sense; it can be transmitted in a philosophical and practical manner that provides the practitioners with a sense of mission that is part of an ongoing historical movement. Practitioners who experience supervision from this perspective can be inspired in a way that will make them more effective and more immune to the despair, disillusionment, and isolation that erode pride in social work professionalism" (Munson, 2002, p. 92). Without this sense of mission, we shall become the "unfaithful angels" who abandoned the mission of social work and who were criticized by Specht and Courtney (1994).

DEFINITIONS OF SOCIAL WORK SUPERVISION

There are three approaches to defining social work supervision: normative, empirical, and pragmatic. The focus of the following discussion is on organizational supervision in the social work field, which should not be confused with fieldwork supervision for social work students or with clinical supervision for counselors.

1. The Normative Approach

The normative approach searches for a norm or standard, and focuses on two basic questions: (1) What should supervision be? and (2) What should the supervisor do? In response to these two questions, many scholars have defined supervision in terms of its administrative and educational functions, with the emphasis varying from author to author (Erera & Lazar, 1994a; Kadushin & Harkness, 2002; Shulman, 1995). For example, Barker (1995) defined social work supervision as "an administrative and educational process used extensively in social agencies to help social workers further develop and refine their skills and to provide quality assurance for the clients. . . (p. 371). Supervision is perceived as an interactional process in which a supervisor assists and directs the practice of the supervisee through teaching, administration, and helping (Dublin, 1989; Kennedy & Keitner, 1970; Munson, 2002; Payne, 1979; Tsui & Ho, 1997). This method of defining social work supervision focuses on ideas and ideals. However, this definition may not reflect the daily practice of supervision.

When we examine the objectives of social work supervision, the widely accepted short-term objective is to improve the worker's capacity to do the job effectively by providing a good work environment, professional knowledge, practice skills, and emotional support

(Kadushin & Harkness, 2002; Munson, 2002). The ultimate objective is to provide effective and efficient service to clients by ensuring the satisfactory job performance and professional competence of front-line social workers (Gitterman, 1972; Harkness & Hensley, 1991; Harkness & Poertner, 1989; Kadushin & Harkness, 2002; Watson, 1973). Therefore, supervision is an important and integral component of social work practice in human service organizations. The normative approach, however, is not concerned with what is going on in the field. It focuses on what supervision should be and aims at.

2. The Empirical Approach

For those who take the empirical approach, the major question is, What does the supervisor really do? Attempts to answer this question involve collecting empirical data about the roles, styles, and behavior of social work supervisors (Kadushin, 1974, 1991, 1992b, 1992c; Ko, 1987; Munson, 2002; Parsloe & Stevenson, 1978; Poertner & Rapp, 1983; Shulman, 1982, 1993; Tsui, 2001). After an extensive review of the existing practice of supervision in the social work field, Kadushin (1974, 1992b, 1992c) concluded that the supervisor is a member of the administrative staff offering an indirect service, which includes administrative, educational, and supportive functions. Kadushin and Harkness (2002) described the components of each supervisory function in detail. They recognized that the administrative, educational, and supportive functions overlap. However, there are specific problems and goals associated with each function. Administrative supervision focuses on the correct, effective, and appropriate implementation of organizational policy and regulations. The aim of educational supervision is to equip frontline social workers with the necessary values, knowledge, and skills to complete the job. Supportive supervision enhances the job satisfaction and staff morale of frontline social workers.

Like Kadushin, Austin (1981) classified supervisory roles. He established four areas of specialization: direct services, organization and administration, training, and personnel management. This role set reflects the administrative, educational, supportive, and personnel-related functions of social work supervision. However, these roles may conflict with each other. For example, data collected in Israel show an incompatibility between administrative and educational functions. Erera and Lazar (1994a) suggested that these functions should be handled separately by different people: an administrative supervisor and an external professional consultant. Miller (1987) maintained that supervisors play an important role in an organization's efforts to link service activities with professional standards, political support, and financial constraints. Williams (1988) suggested that supervisors have a range of alternative roles instead of a single role.

A task analysis conducted by Poertner and Rapp (1983) revealed that supervisors focus on their administrative roles (63 percent of their tasks), while educational and supportive activities represent only 20 percent of their duties. However, Harkness and Poertner (1989) suggested that these empirical, descriptive definitions are of limited value. They fail to distinguish sufficiently between social work supervisors and frontline social work practitioners. In fact, it is a long journey from conducting empirical research to building up an empirically grounded theory of social work supervision.

3. The Pragmatic Approach

The pragmatic approach does not focus on providing a formal definition of social work supervision; instead its aim is to provide action guidelines for social work supervisors and to identify the functions and tasks of social work supervision. For the past five decades, functional definitions of supervision have been based on the balance of administrative, educational, and supportive functions. Debates have largely focused on which function—administrative or educational—ranks first in the hierarchy, with supportive almost always relegated to third place.

Since the 1950s, the compatibility of the administrative function and the educational function has been questioned (Arndt, 1955; Austin, 1956; Berkowitz, 1952; Erera & Lazar, 1994a; Feldman, 1950; Hester, 1951). Those who advocate a balance of the three functions of social work supervision (Kadushin & Harkness, 2002; Payne, 1994; Wilson, 1981) believe that, although the various functions represent divergent organizational boundaries as well as distinct domains of knowledge and skills, they are not only congruent but also complementary. Other researchers (Austin, 1956; Erera & Lazar, 1994a; Miller, 1987) argue that there is a built-in incompatibility between administrative and educational functions and that it is better to separate the two in order to achieve greater supervisory effectiveness. Social work supervisors should focus on the administrative function and leave the educational function to consultants.

While neither side of the argument has been proven empirically (Erera & Lazar, 1994a), the research points to an interesting gap between the real and the ideal, between what supervisors actually spend most of their time doing and what they consider to be most important (Middleman & Rhodes, 1985; Payne, 1994). Although supervisors spend most of their time on administrative functions (Poertner & Rapp, 1983), they rank the educational function as the most important aspect of social work supervision (Kadushin, 1992c).

In the 1950s, Austin (1957) asked three fundamental questions about the supervisory functions that are still valid today. First, can the supervisor continue to combine the administrative and educational functions in view of increased specialization? Second, if the administrative and educational functions are separated and assigned to different people, can a new effective division of labor be achieved? Third, can professional social workers assume more responsibility for their own work and take the initiative to seek consultation rather than receive continual supervision passively? Unfortunately, although much effort has been directed toward resolving the conflicts among the different functions of supervision, and many alternative typologies have been suggested (see, e.g., Middleman & Rhodes, 1985; Rich, 1993; Rivas, 1991), Austin's questions remain unanswered almost five decades later.

PERSONAL SUPERVISION, PROFESSIONAL SUPERVISION, AND ORGANIZATIONAL SUPERVISION

Social work supervisors in human service organizations have three roles. Their supervision is intended to provide comprehensive monitoring, in the form of personal supervision, professional supervision, and organizational supervision. Personal supervision focuses on the emotional requirements of the social worker in the work setting. In the process of personal supervision, the supervisee is treated as a friend of the supervisor, and there is a primary, informal, and personal relationship between the supervisor and the supervisee. Professional supervision focuses on equipping the social worker with the required professional values, knowledge, and skills necessary for problem solving and professional growth. In the process of professional supervision, the supervisee is treated as a developing helping professional and social work supervision is perceived as a means of professional growth. In some human service organizations, social work supervision is viewed as a kind of staff development activity. Organizational supervision focuses on administrative aspects, emphasizing the quality of the service delivery and the efficiency of the intervention. This focus reflects the organization's accountability to the community and funding sources. From the perspective of organizational supervision, the supervisee is an employee. This view helps to distinguish social work supervision from consultation. Between the supervisor and the supervisee, there is a significant difference in the hierarchy of power, which may not be found in the relationship between consultant and consultee.

THE OBJECTIVES OF SOCIAL WORK SUPERVISION

After examining what social work supervision is, we must also consider what social work supervision strives for. As Kadushin and Harkness (2002) observed, the ultimate long-term objective of social work supervision is to provide efficient and effective services to clients. In the short term, the objective of administrative supervision is to provide frontline social workers with a context that permits them to do their job effectively. Educational supervision aims to improve the staff's capacity to do the job effectively, by helping workers develop professionally and maximizing their practice knowledge and skills. The goal of supportive supervision is to ensure that staff social workers feel good about their job.

Payne (1994) identified 17 specific objectives of social work supervision in the social work literature. These objectives can be divided into three groups: those for clients, those for supervisees, and those for supervisors and management. First, supervision should ensure that clients receive maximum benefits and prohibit inappropriate staff responses to clients. Second, supervision enables supervisees to deliver more effective care, get a second opinion, raise concerns about their own intervention, pursue professional development, receive feedback, deal with their own feelings, and enhance their own self-management. From the supervisor's perspective, supervision is used to maintain standards and morale in service units; monitor workload levels; review and plan interventions; maintain objectivity; provide critical analysis; keep senior staff informed about the performance of frontline staff; ensure court orders, statutory requirements, and other obligations are discharged; and maintain good standards of professional performance.

From the preceding discussion, it is clear that there are many ways of defining social work supervision. Each approach will result in its own definition. However, we may, at least, form a comprehensive picture of what social work supervision is and what it should be.

2

Theoretical Models of Social Work Supervision

MODELS OF SOCIAL WORK SUPERVISION

A model is a simplified picture that acts as an aid to understanding reality (Dechert, 1965; Galt & Smith, 1976). Sergiovanni (1983) suggested that model building should be concerned with the ideals, the contexts, the components, and the action guidelines. Models clarify the supervisory process and are, thus, useful tools. Because models are specific and flexible, they are also easily modified and tested (Bernard & Goodyear, 1992). In supervisory practice, models can provide a common language for the supervisor and the supervisee. Of course, it may be possible to learn how to supervise through imitation or by trial and error. However, without a model, a supervisor may not be able to conceptualize the process of supervision in a holistic manner.

As mentioned in Chapter 1, social work supervision is almost as old as social work practice itself. Although its format and focus have varied over the years, supervision has assumed and maintained a unique and important position in the social work field (Waldfogel, 1983). Social work supervision has been identified as one of the most significant factors in determining the job satisfaction levels of frontline social workers. It has also been cited as a crucial determinant of service quality (Harkness, 1995; Harkness & Hensley, 1991; Harkness & Poertner, 1989; Kadushin & Harkness, 2002).

Scholars have noted that there are numerous models of supervision in the helping professions (Bruce & Austin, 2000; Latting, 1986; Lowy, 1983; White & Russell, 1995). Rich (1993) even went so far as to call the field a "supervisory jungle." Like theories of management, which, according to Koontz (1961, 1980), have created a "theory jungle," models of social work supervision have proliferated. However, there is no empirically grounded theory of social work supervision available to the social work profession (Kadushin & Harkness, 2002; Middleman & Rhodes, 1985; Munson, 2002; Tsui, 1997b; White & Russell, 1995).

Many scholars have borrowed theories from other social sciences to describe, explain, and predict the behavior of the supervisor and the supervisee in the supervisory process (Kadushin & Harkness, 2002; Munson, 2002; Shulman, 1993; Tsui, 1997a). From the late 1800s to the 1950s, the major trend was to borrow theories from psychology, particularly from Freudian psychotherapy (Bernard & Goodyear, 1992; Munson, 1981). Since the 1950s, scholars have also turned to the works of sociologists to provide a conceptual background. For example, Munson (1976, 1979a, 1979b, 1979e) conceptualized supervision according to Merton's role set and interaction theory. Shulman (1982, 1993) used the framework created by Schwartz to develop the interactional supervision model. In its daily practice, social work supervision also borrowed from other helping professions such as medicine, nursing, and education (Rich, 1993).

Rich (1993) reviewed all existing models of supervision and constructed an integrated model that encompasses all the perspectives and components of supervision. This integrated model features six areas of classification: facilitative environment, supervisory relationship, structural elements, supervisory skills, provision of learning experience, and supervisory roles. In each category, several important elements are identified and described in detail. First, a facilitative environment is a safe, open, autonomous, interactive, sharing environment in which the supervisee has strong motivation to learn and the supervisor provides adequate support and is attentive to the needs of the staff. Second, the supervisory relationship relies on intimacy, trust, respect, and empathy. Third, the structure for supervision must have clear goals and specific expectations, consistency of supervisory leadership, reinforcement for learning, positive feedback, and case-oriented supervision sessions. Fourth, essential supervisory skills include technical skills, listening skills, communication skills, analytical skills, elaboration skills, and interpretive skills. Fifth, principles of adult learning apply to the supervisory process. Supervisees should be viewed as active learners who require didactic instruction, modeling, experiential learning, and guided practice, and shared experiences are adopted. Finally, the supervisor has to play the roles of counselor, teacher, consultant, colleague, mentor, and evaluator, as required. Rich's model provides a useful guide that encourages supervisors to do their job more effectively.

Holloway (1995) constructed a "systems approach to supervision" (SAS) model that emphasizes the interrelationships among the various subsystems of clinical supervision. McKitrick and Garrison (1992) suggested an outline for theory building that facilitates the construction of a practice model of supervision. The model provides a detailed inventory of action guidelines for clarifying the philosophy, context, approach, process, supervisor-supervisee relationship, and outcome of supervision. Although such models are derived from the practice of clinical supervision, they provide a useful frame of reference for the formulation of the conditions and components of a model of social work supervision. In this chapter, the models of social work supervision will be reviewed.

In the social work field, there are various interpretations of the term "model of supervision." I have identified 11 models of supervision under five categories in the field of social work (Table 2.1).

Practice Theory as a Supervision Model

Scholars, noting that clinical supervisors adopt therapy theories as models of supervision, have cited various reasons for this development (Liddle & Saba, 1983; Olsen & Stern, 1990; Storm & Heath, 1985). First, given the dearth of formal supervision theory, it may be an alternative to develop supervision models based on the structure of practice theory. Second, theories of therapy are relatively well developed. For example, the assumptions, components, and contents are specifically defined. Third, therapy has been clearly described in existing literature; it is easy for the supervisors and the frontline social workers to search and digest. Fourth, therapy theories offer concrete guidance on practice skills. Fifth, the use of therapy as a model of supervision allows us to build on what is already known. There are ready-to-use guides. Finally, because the formats of therapy and supervision are similar, there is less resistance on the part of social workers. For example, solution-focused therapy provides a structured

Table 2.1   Models of Social Work Supervision

Name of Model	Sources
1. Practice Theory as Model	Bernard & Goodyear, 1992; Liddle & Saba, 1983; Olsen & Stern, 1990; Russell, Crinnings, & Lent, 1984; Storm & Heath, 1985
2. Structural-Functional Models	
a. Supervisory function model	Erera & Lazar, 1994a; Kadushin & Harkness, 2002
b. Integrative model	Gitterman, 1972; Lowy, 1983
c. Models of authority	Munson, 1976, 1979a, 1981, 1993, 2002
3. Agency Models	
a. Casework model	Kadushin, 1974, 1992b; Ko, 1987
b. Group supervision model	Kadushin & Harkness, 2002; Sales & Navarre, 1970; Watson, 1973
c. Peer supervision model	Watson, 1973
d. Team service delivery model	Kadushin & Harkness, 2002
e. Autonomous practice	Barretta-Herman, 1993; Epstein, 1973; Kadushin, 1974; Kadushin & Harkness, 2002; Kutzik, 1977; Rock, 1990; Veeder, 1990; Watson, 1973; Wax, 1979
4. Interactional Process Model	Gitterman, 1972; Gitterman & Miller, 1977; Hart, 1982; Latting, 1986; Shulman, 1993; Stoltenberg, 1981; Worthington, 1984
5. Feminist Partnership Model	Chernesky, 1986; Hipp & Munson, 1995

format and clearly scheduled stages for helping the client. The efforts are focused on step-by-step progress within a limited period of time, instead of lengthy discussions of problems.

The parallel linkage between therapy and supervision is called "isomorphism," which occurs when two complex structures are mapped onto each other. For each part of one structure, there is a corresponding counterpart in the other (Bernard & Goodyear, 1992). There are, however, some drawbacks to an isomorphic relationship between therapy and supervision (Russell, Crinnings, & Lent, 1984). First of all, it inhibits the development of a formal theory specific and unique to supervision. Second, it also hinders attempts to view supervision in an integrative manner. Third, therapy theorists often fail to operationalize their hypotheses and constructs for verification and testing. Finally, the dependence on therapy theories suggests that the profession has not reached a mature stage: one of the indicators of the maturity of the practice of social work supervision is the emergence of models that are independent of therapy (Bernard & Goodyear, 1992).

Structural-Functional Models

The structural-functional models of social work supervision focus on the objectives, functions, and structure of supervision. Three models can be identified: the supervisory function model, the integrative model, and the model of authority.

Supervisory function model

This model emphasizes the administrative, educational, and supportive functions of supervision (Erera & Lazar, 1994a; Kadushin & Harkness, 2002). Each supervisory function has its own set of problems and goals. The priorities of administrative supervision are to adhere to the agency policies and procedures and to implement them effectively. Educational supervision addresses the staff's level of professional knowledge and skills, and aims to improve their competence in professional practice. The supportive-expressive function is fulfilled by taking care of workload, stress, and morale, in order to improve the job satisfaction and motivation of the social workers (Kadushin & Harkness, 2002; Shulman, 1993, 1995). The supervisory function model provides clear boundaries and directions for supervisors. For each function, there is a set of tasks to complete. It is easy to understand and implement.

Integrative model

Gitterman (1972) suggested three social work supervision models: an organization-oriented model, a worker-centered model, and an integrative model. The organization-oriented model focuses on the client outcome: social work supervision is used as an administrative mechanism to ensure the result of human service delivery. The worker-centered model emphasizes job satisfaction and professional development of frontline staff: social work supervision is conceived as a tool for the development of frontline social workers. It is assumed that competent and dedicated staff members will enhance the effective outcomes of human services. Gitterman (1972) preferred the integrative model, which is a combination of the other two models and is, therefore, more comprehensive. He maintained that the integrative model is detailed enough to illustrate the dynamic aspect of the organic link between the supervisor and the supervisee and yet remains simple to use. It covers "knowing," "feeling," and "doing." Both the supervisor and the supervisee have functions to perform and roles to play.

Lowy (1983) also formulated three models. The work-oriented model ensures that the practitioner's work is carried out in accordance with the demands of the organization and professional values. The theory- and method-oriented model emphasizes schools of thought and methods. The learning model focuses on the educational aspects of supervision. None of these models exists in a pure form—supervisors always use them in an integrative manner. However, they are useful for conceptualization. As Lowy (1983) pointed out, if social work supervision is to have a greater impact on the practice of frontline social workers than providing piecemeal guidelines for action, a move toward theory building is necessary. Such a move would generate significant and meaningful discussion about issues affecting supervision and its impact on social work theory and practice.

Models of authority

Munson (1976, 1979a, 1979b, 1981, 1993, 2002) dealt primarily with the use of authority in social work supervision. As authority is built into the supervisory relationship, the supervisor should use it to meet the needs of the supervisees. Munson developed two models to represent the ways that authority is used: the sanction model and the competence model. According to the sanction model, the authority of supervisors comes from the top management of the organization. Supervisors represent the authority inherent in their administrative position based on the agency's sanction. The competence model is based on professional authority derived from the supervisor's own knowledge and skills. This means that the supervisor has the skill "competence" to handle the required job effectively. Munson (1979b, 1981) conducted a study of 64 supervisors and 65 supervisees.

Significant variations in the levels of interaction, supervision and job satisfaction, and sense of accomplishment were found according to the source of the supervisor's authority. When Munson (1979b, 1981) compared these variables, he found that the competence model is more effective in creating a high level of interaction, satisfaction with the supervisory process, sense of accomplishment, and job satisfaction. The research shows that the competence model of authority is more effective than the sanction model in enhancing supervisor-supervisee interaction and job satisfaction.

Agency Models

In human service organizations, supervision models often reflect the level of control exercised by the agency (Kadushin & Harkness, 2002; Skidmore, 1995; Watson, 1973). At one extreme is the casework model, which is based on a high level of administrative accountability. At the other extreme is the autonomous practice model where there is high degree of professional autonomy (Epstein, 1973; Rock, 1990; Veeder, 1990). Between these extremes are the group supervision model (Brown & Bourne, 1996; Getzel, Goldberg, & Salmon, 1971; Kaplan, 1991; Kaslow, 1972; Shulman, 1993), the peer supervision model (Skidmore, 1995), and the team service delivery model (Payne & Scott, 1982).

The casework model

The theories of social work supervision have been greatly influenced by the theories of social work practice, especially social casework practice (Kadushin & Harkness, 2002). This may account for the fact that the format of supervision looks like that of casework intervention. The casework model consists of a supervisor and a supervisee in a one-on-one relationship; the role of the supervisor encompasses the administrative, educational, and supportive functions. This is the most widely adopted model of supervision, especially for inexperienced workers (Kadushin, 1974, 1992b; Ko, 1987). For example, Kadushin (1992b) found in a national survey that individual meetings are the principal format of supervision sessions for 83 percent of supervisors and 79 percent of supervisees. The session is usually scheduled once a week. On average, it takes longer than one hour but less than two hours. Supervisors tend to use the one-on-one tutorial method they learned from their fieldwork supervisors in schools of social work (Tsui, 2001).

The group supervision model

After the casework model, the group supervision model is the most popular model of supervision in social work. Group supervision is often used as a supplement to, rather than a substitute for, individual supervision (Kadushin, 1992b; Ko, 1987). As defined by Kadushin and Harkness (2002), group supervision uses a group setting to fulfill the responsibilities of social work supervision. The primary and ultimate objectives of group supervision are the same as those for individual supervision. However, the group setting saves time and human resources. In addition, there are more teaching and learning experiences available in the group context, because the participants share their difficulties and experiences.

In a group session, the supervisor functions as a group leader, encouraging staff members to share their difficulties and their insights. As this model focuses on the common needs of the staff members, the workers in the group cannot be too diverse in terms of their levels of professional training or practice experience (Watson, 1973). Within the group, the balance of power between the leader and team members is more equitable than in other supervisory models. The staff feel that they have greater freedom to communicate their dissatisfaction to the supervisor in group supervision sessions (Kadushin & Harkness, 2002). The members are exposed to a wide variety of learning experiences in a relatively comfortable environment, and emotional support is provided by the group not only by the supervisor. Of course, group supervision is sometimes ineffective in handling specific individual needs or problems, and it can lead to peer competition. Thus, the success of the group supervision model depends on the skills of the supervisor, the motivation of staff members, and the culture of the organization.

Brown and Bourne (1996) identified seven kinds of decisions that supervisors using group supervision must make. They include boundaries, tasks, structure, roles, type of facilitation, the supervisory relationship, and methods. First, boundary decisions are concerned with the duration, frequency, membership, rules, confidentiality, and defining characteristics of group meetings. Second, group supervision performs various tasks Usually, there are four general tasks: providing emotional support, providing practical consultation, team building, and addressing agency issues. The supervisor needs to consult with the group on the weighting of various tasks. The clearer the vision is, the more effective the group supervision will be. Third, regarding the structure of the group supervision, the members have made decisions at the outset concerning use of time, choice of content, pattern of participation, and kinds of activities. Fourth, the roles of members should be differentiated. Of course, the supervisor plays the role of the group leader, while the other members assume other responsibilities (record keeper, facilitator, resource person, etc.). This division of labor may be based on interest, skills, or seniority, or may be accomplished by simple rotation. Fifth, decisions must be made about the type of facilitation offered—whether it is maintaining the structure, clarifying the content, or enabling the process. Sixth, it should be clearly understood who is supervising whom. There are four possible patterns: supervision of individuals within a group by the supervisor, supervision of individuals by the group, supervision of the group as a whole by the supervisor, and supervision of the group by themselves. Finally, many methods can be adopted in the group supervision session, including group discussion, working in small groups (e.g., dyads or triads), role playing, structural exercises, games, and projective exercises (e.g., artwork and audiovisual presentations) (Brown & Bourne, 1996, p. 162).

Of course, there are advantages and disadvantages to group supervision. As Brown and Bourne (1996) pointed out, there is a wider variety of learning experiences to share in the group supervision session. The frontline social workers may receive support from peers, and, as a result, they may feel more secure. Group sessions also provide an opportunity to compare one's own experiences and practices with others. This process fosters team spirit, group cohesion, and the "we" identity. The supervisor acts as a group leader and identifies the potential problems of the work team. There is a higher level of differentiation of roles within a group. In a group setting, peer influence may make behavioral change more likely. Supervisees can learn from the supervisor, both directly and as a role model. There is a progression from dependence on the supervisor, through interdependence among peers, to independence. A group allows greater empowerment through lateral teaching, learning, and support of peers (Brown & Bourne, 1996, p. 162).

However, as Brown and Bourne (1996, p. 162) cautioned, group supervision focuses on issues that have relevance to the largest number of group members. Specific and urgent needs cannot be handled immediately. The group may also stimulate sibling rivalry and peer competition. It is often difficult to incorporate a new staff member into a supervisory group. In many cases, it may seem easier to opt out of the responsibility to engage in exploration, problem solving, and decision making. Critical feedback can be inhibiting if there is a lack of confidence. The supervisor is more exposed and requires greater self-assurance in group situations than in individual sessions. Comments and interventions that assist one member may create problems for other members. Supervisors may find it difficult to get back on track should the group follow an unproductive route. They must have a clear grasp of group interactions, group dynamics, and individual behavior in the group context. They must be able to focus on both the individual and the group. Finally, conformity to group norms may be harmful to the creativity and productivity of the work team.

The peer supervision model

Peer supervision does not rely on a designated supervisor; all staff participate equally (Hardcastle, 1991; Watson, 1973). Staff members take responsibility for their own work. There are no regular individual supervision sessions between the supervisor and the supervisee; instead, there are regular case conferences of all staff members and collegial consultation is common. Peer supervision encourages the staff to be more sensitive to the needs and difficulties of others by creating an atmosphere of mutual help and sharing. As Hardcastle (1991) observed, the peer supervision model may increase the worker's responsibility, accountability, and authority. The major deter-minant of this model's success is the worker's experience. For exam-ple, it may not be a good choice if all staff members are inexperienced: the participants would not have adequate knowledge for useful dis-cussions. In addition, the nature of the service setting, client vulnera-bility, and agency liability must be taken into account. Hardcastle (1991) listed the factors that should determine the structure of supervision:

(i)   The more complex and volatile the worker's technologies, the greater the need for close supervision of the worker.

(ii) The less predictable and reliable the worker's technologies, and the less reliable and clear the cause-effect relationships between the worker's technologies and the outcomes, the greater the need for close supervision of the worker.

(iii) The less visible the worker's technologies, the greater the need for close supervision of the worker.

(iv) The less reversible the worker's technologies, and the greater the impact and risk of the technologies on the clients, the greater the need for close supervision of the worker.

(v) The more routinized the worker's technologies, the less need for close supervision of the worker.

(vi) The more interdependent the technologies of line workers, and the more a line worker needs other line worker technologies to complete the task, the greater the need for close supervision and coordination.

(vii) The less experienced the line worker is in the technologies, the greater the need for close supervision of the worker.

(viii) The more experienced and knowledgeable the line worker is in the organization's protocols and procedures, the less need for close supervision of the line worker.

(ix) The more turbulent the work environment, and the greater the risk to the agency, the greater the need for close supervision of the worker (Hardcastle, 1991, p. 74).

An alternative to this model of supervision, which evolved from the peer group model, is the "tandem" model (Watson, 1973). Tandem supervision occurs when two frontline social workers, one with professional experience and the other relatively junior, consult each other apart from the peer group. They are like the two wheels, big and small, of a classic tandem bicycle. Both are steering in the same direction. In professional practice, both are practitioners, and neither is designated the supervisor. In tandem, they meet occasionally and informally to discuss their assignments and working experiences. Tandem members arrange to go on vacation at different times so that they can cover each other's work, thereby exposing themselves to learning opportunities. However, tandem members are not accountable for each other's job performance. The main objective is to share professional knowledge and skills.

The tandem model is similar to the mentorship programs that are common in other human service fields, such as education and nursing. A mentor is someone who takes a personal interest in another's career and acts as a guide or sponsor. It is an interpersonal helping relationship between two individuals (the mentor and the protégé) at different stages in the process of professional development, and it is undertaken on a voluntary and self-motivated basis (Campion & Goldfinch, 1981; Collins, 1994; Kelly, 2001; Ragins & Scandura, 1994). Chao (1998) argued that, although there is no clear conceptual definition of mentorship, four basic mentoring functions can be identified: socialization, technological assistance, career development, and emotional support (Chao, 1998; Kelly, 2001). Socialization helps the protégé to adjust to the organization and ensures that the protégé understands the organizational culture, written and unwritten. Technological assistance through direct teaching or through the provision of challenging assignments builds up the protégé's technical skills. The protégé's need to develop competence and demonstrate specific skills is often complemented by the mentor's need to become more of a generalist. Career advancement includes information about opportunities, letters of reference, and sponsorship for advancement to a particular position. Emotional support encompasses acceptance, supportive criticism, and timely encouragement (Kelly, 2001, p. 20).

The team service delivery model

In the team service delivery model, the supervisor plays the role of team leader. There are no regular supervision sessions. The team focuses on the work itself and contributes to the decision-making process, although the team leader has the final say. The responsibility for work assignment, performance monitoring, and professional development belongs to the team (Kadushin & Harkness, 2002; Payne & Scott, 1982).

The autonomous practice model

A movement in favor of more professional autonomy for social workers has coincided with the maturation of social work as a profession. It is one of the natural steps of the developmental process, much like the creation of professional training institutes, the formulation of a professional code of ethics, and the establishment of professional associations. The advocates of professional autonomy argue that, for experienced and professionally trained practitioners, there is no need to provide one-on-one, face-to-face, direct supervision (Epstein, 1973; Kutzik, 1977; Veeder, 1990). Veeder (1990) summarized the findings of a survey of MSW students who were taking a course in supervisory management. The respondents felt that close supervision is essential to new and inexperienced social workers, but not to experienced ones. Experienced social workers may occasionally seek the advice of other professionals, if required.

Assuming the frontline social workers have an MSW and have been working in the same service setting, the amount of time that constitutes "experience" ranges from two to six years (Kadushin & Harkness, 2002; Veeder, 1990; Wax, 1979). Epstein (1973) argued that autonomous practice is possible in the social work field. Its two pre-conditions are the decentralization of bureaucratic authority and the abandonment of the obligatory teaching process as a means of controlling professional behavior. These developments would, in turn, make social work practice more flexible, although administrators would still regularly monitor and appraise the staff.

A national survey conducted by Kadushin (1992b) in the United States showed that social workers accept the administrative functions of their supervisors, but that experienced workers complain about educational supervision if it is provided by inexperienced supervisors. Mandell (1973) found that prolonged individual supervision of social workers has a tendency to stifle creativity and innovation. In autonomous practice, staff members are not assigned supervisors. The staff are "self-directed" (Rock, 1990) and responsible for their own professional practice. In addition, they must take the initiative to pursue continuing education if they wish to enhance their own professional development. It has been argued that trained workers should be allowed to assume responsibility for their work and professional development after a number of years of supervised practice. In fact, this kind of professional autonomy has long been found in private practice.

Barretta-Herman (1993) proposed an autonomous model of supervision for licensed social work practitioners. A licensed practitioner is assumed to be well trained and experienced. Thus, the primary responsibility for continual professional development and accountability rests with the practitioner, not the supervisor. The supervisor only plays the role of facilitator. Group supervision is adopted as the primary mode of supervision. The supervisor is no longer "super" in terms of knowledge and skills. Supervisors assume the role of experts to help supervisees gain insight into their practice. The supervisor uses supervision to encourage purposeful reflection and provide critical feedback, and creates a challenging work environment for the frontline social workers. The supervisory relationship is interactive, interdependent, and more evenly balanced. For the frontline social workers, the supervisory relationship provides an opportunity to reflect on intervention processes, outcomes, and professional growth. As Veeder (1990) pointed out, however, this method blunts the self-accountability of the truly autonomous professional. Also, supervisors must be aware of professional and legal liabilities when they adopt this model.

In his article "Differential Supervision" (1973), Watson observed that the goal of supervision is to provide better service to the clients by helping social workers become more competent and motivated in their jobs. Instead of adopting a single model as the supermodel, Watson maintained that a variety of supervisory models should be provided as options to meet the different needs of staff members. These models would take into account variations in organizational structure, including service settings and the developmental stages of the frontline workers.

Interactional Process Models

Interactional process models focus on the interaction between the supervisor and the supervisee in the supervisory process. Latting (1986) proposed an adaptive supervision model that identifies four interactional patterns between the supervisor and the supervisee. According to this model, instrumental behavior is appropriate for administrative and educational functions, while expressive behavior is more suitable to the supportive function. Supervisors can take a proactive or a reflective approach to their expressive behavior: "In the proactive mode, the supervisor tries to influence the worker's attitudes and behavior in the work setting. For example, the supervisor may take the form of coaching, providing theory, putting the worker's unspoken feelings into words, directing the worker towards other sources of help and information, and strategic questioning. In the reflective mode, the worker takes the lead in the interaction; the supervisor becomes more of a sounding board. The focus is less on task and process direction in the supervisory content and more on helping the worker to understand the foundation of his or her assumptions and actions" (Latting, 1986, p. 20). If supervisors adopt a proactive attitude, they encourage, or collaborate with, supervisees. On the other hand, supervisors may take a reflective approach wherein they instruct their supervisees and require them to take the initiative. The appropriate use of each approach is crucial to the effectiveness of supervisory practice.

There are two types of interactional process models: the developmental model and the growth-oriented model. According to the developmental model, supervision focuses on the stages of development of the supervisory process, necessary for supervisees to acquire the skills of their professional practice (Hart, 1982; Stoltenberg, 1981; Worthington, 1984). For example, at the beginning of a supervisory relationship with new staff, the supervisor may need to focus on orienting the staff to the service unit. At a later stage, the frequency of the supervision sessions may be reduced in order to allow the staff autonomy in direct practice. The second type, the growth-oriented model of supervision, is tailored to the supervisees. It focuses on the enhancement of the supervisees' understanding of their personal self and professional self. The supervisor shifts the emphasis from service delivery to the development of the self, which is a prerequisite to the development of professional helping relationships. The growth-oriented model ensures that frontline staff express their feelings, have personal insights, and develop their personalities (Gitterman, 1972).

The Feminist Partnership Model

As in other areas of social work practice, feminism has had a significant impact on social work supervision (Gross, 2000; Parton, 2003). Some feminists are critical of the traditional social work supervision model and see interminable supervision, administrative control, and the power hierarchy of the supervisor-supervisee relationship as manifestations of a patriarchal model of power.

Scholars (Chernesky, 1986; Hipp & Munson, 1995) have proposed an alternative—a feminist partnership model that assumes the social worker can be self-directing, self-disciplined, and self-regulating. The relationship between the supervisor and the supervisee would be reconstructed as a sharing relationship between equal partners. The hierarchy of power would be reconceptualized as collegial affiliation. Direct supervision as a performance-monitoring mechanism would be replaced by indirect mechanisms such as group norms and peer approval. The advocates of the feminist partnership model claim that it is more compatible with the values of the social work profession than the traditional authority model. Of course, this model of supervision is the subject of heated debate and there are often political issues involved in specific societies.

THE STATE OF THE ART OF SOCIAL WORK SUPERVISION

The preceding review of the 11 existing models of social work supervision reveals that none of them addresses the impact of the greater environment. They focus instead on professional autonomy, supervisory functions, the supervisory relationship, supervisory authority, and the format of supervision. Because social workers are also members of a socio-cultural system, the values, beliefs, and norms of their society have considerable influence on their behavior. The models discussed in this chapter neglect the importance of this influence. In addition, the models do not build on each other. Each scholar describes certain aspects of social work supervision, but none encompasses the larger framework of the cultural environment. It is very important to examine supervision in its cultural context so that it can be explored in a comprehensive manner. The four parties involved in the supervisory process—the supervisee, the supervisor, the agency, and the client—are all strongly influenced by the culture of their society.

3

Constructing a Comprehensive Model of Social Work Supervision Within a Cultural Context

I n this chapter, a comprehensive model of social work supervision will be generated from the existing literature.

PHILOSOPHY AND PRINCIPLES

A model is an abstract of reality. In a professional context, models of practice are constructed on the basis of assumptions and principles that reflect the underlying philosophy of the profession. A model of social work supervision is no exception: its philosophical base is the ideals and beliefs of social work supervisors. A close examination of the theoretical and empirical bases of supervision reveals seven basic principles that govern model building. These principles are as follows:

1. Supervision is an interpersonal transaction between two or more persons. The premise of supervision is that an experienced and competent supervisor helps the supervisee and ensures the quality of service to clients (Kadushin, 1992a).

2. The work of the supervisee is related to the agency objectives through the supervisor (Kadushin & Harkness, 2002; Shulman, 1995).

3. In this interpersonal transaction, there is a use of authority (the organizational administrative function), an exchange of information and ideas (the professional/educational function), and an expression of emotion (the emotional/supportive function) (Munson, 1976, 1979a, 1979b, 1981, 1983, 1993, 2002).

4. As part of the indirect practice of social work, supervision reflects the professional values of social work (Kadushin & Harkness, 2002; Munson, 1993; Shulman, 1993; Tsui, 1997a).

5. The supervisor monitors job performance; conveys professional values, knowledge, and skills; and provides emotional support to the supervisee (Kadushin & Harkness, 2002; Tsui, 1998a).

6. In order to reflect both the short- and long-term objectives of supervision, the criteria for evaluating supervisory effectiveness include staff satisfaction with supervision, job accomplishment, and client outcomes (Harkness, 1995; Harkness & Hensley, 1991; Kadushin & Harkness, 2002).

7. From a holistic point of view, supervision involves four parties: the agency, the supervisor, the supervisee, and the client (Kadushin & Harkness, 2002; Shulman, 1993; Tsui & Ho, 1997).

Social work supervision is an enabling process. It is also a mirror of direct social work practice. As a result, social work supervision is a process that parallels direct social work intervention. The principles of social work supervision enable social workers to actualize their vision and articulate the mission of social work, in order to enhance professional competence, staff morale, and job satisfaction. Through this process, the quality of service delivery to clients will be safeguarded and improved.

Interpersonal Transactions

Social work supervision is a process of interpersonal communication between the supervisor and the supervisee, focused on a particular job in an organizational context. It is a very intensive process that takes into account the diversity of perspectives within a specific culture. The human being is a complex social animal, and social workers are very complex human beings. Social workers learn a great deal about human behavior from their academic training, continuing education, and practice. It is not unusual for social workers to achieve their goals through sophisticated interpersonal transactions.

Based on the values of social work and the nature of social workers, the first principle of an effective supervisor is to be a real person, not a "super" adviser or a "superficial" adviser, in the supervisory process. In fact, many effective supervisors who are competent and popular are not superior or wiser. They are just doing their job with a humanistic attitude: they maintain the principles of social work, consider the benefit of clients their top priority, and, at the same time, take care of their staff's needs and feelings.

Social workers are trained to be observant and sensitive, and are especially so when assessing the motives and behavior of their supervisors. Thus, supervisors should not play power games; they should just be themselves. As time goes by, your supervisees will get to know you. The best role for a supervisee is that of a growing practitioner and an active learner. To provide effective supervision, a supervisor must acknowledge the power hierarchy in the supervisory relationship but assert the supervisee's right to know, to learn, to choose, and to voice alternate opinions. The supervisor-supervisee relationship should not be merely a professional relationship; it requires personal commitment. This is why many supervisors and their supervisees, after a period of collegial cooperation, become lifelong friends.

Fox (1983) suggested 12 action guidelines for supervisors. I have divided them into three categories according to their general functions:

Administrative functions

    i. Be accessible and ready to discuss work.
    ii. Provide ongoing specific feedback.
    iii. Involve workers in setting goals.

Educational functions

    iv. Strengthen links with outside experts.
    v. Motivate the supervisee to become more independent.
    vi. Provide well-organized materials for professional growth.

Supportive functions

    vii. Sustain and stimulate a climate of trust, respect, interest, and support.

   viii. Handle painful material openly, objectively, and directly.

     ix. State honestly when you cannot help or do not know how to proceed.

      x. Empathize with the supervisee's feelings, attitudes, and behavior.

     xi. Recognize the supervisee's frustration, tensions, and anxiety.

   xii. Recognize and reinforce achievement, and reflect on success as well as failure.

As you can see, Fox (1983) emphasized the importance of supportive functions, as they are the key to motivating staff and sustaining morale. As long as the staff are willing to remain in their service units, feel happy about their job, and are motivated to learn, they will perform well on the job.

Relevance to Agency Objectives

Agency objectives outline the direction and expected outcome of the mission of the agency as an institution. Most social workers work in human service organizations as employees; as a result, their job is to fulfill the objectives of the agency. This is reflected in the comprehensive model of social work supervision (Tsui & Ho, 1997). Social workers cannot be directly accountable to clients in an open market because the client, in most cases, is a service consumer but not the bill payer (Tsui & Cheung, 2000a). Thus, frontline social workers are accountable to their supervisors through the supervisory process, while supervisors report to the top management, the executive, and the board members of the agency. The agency is indirectly accountable to clients through funding sources such as the government. The funded agency must fulfill the requirements of various policies and procedures. Of course, this kind of indirect accountability to clients is not ideal. The practice of supervision will be significantly changed when more social workers enter private practice.

Use of Authority, Exchange of Information, and Expression of Feelings

The supervisory process involves use of authority, exchange of information, and expression of feelings. These correspond to the three widely recognized functions of supervision: administrative, educational, and supportive. However, this multipurpose interaction creates conflicting demands on the supervisor. To meet these demands, social work supervision must be not only a practice but also an art. Social work supervision is difficult to teach, which does not mean that it cannot be learned. There are a wide range of principles, strategies, and skills. The basic principle of effective supervision is to be "human." This principle is at the root of social work practice and is upheld by the social work profession as the core of its faith.

From the data provided by focus group sessions that I conducted with 40 experienced social work supervisors in Hong Kong, five guidelines of supervision emerged. First, supervisors should be ethical and dedicated. Second, supervisors should have a sense of professional and social responsibility. Supervisors must maintain a balance between social work values and administrative requirements. Third, supervisors should have a positive attitude toward themselves, their supervisees, and their clients. Fourth, supervisors should be rational and logical. Finally, supervisors should be continuous learners, always ready to refresh their knowledge and skills, seek advice from top management, obtain support from and exchange ideas with colleagues, and benefit from the expertise of external consultants.

A Reflection of Personal and Professional Values

Social work supervision is a close interaction between two or more helping professionals. Naturally, the personal values of the supervisor and the supervisee will affect the process and the result of supervisory practice. However, as both supervisor and supervisee are professional social workers, they have undergone the socialization process inherent in professional training. It is also their obligation to uphold the professional values of social work in their practice. Thus, the supervisory process is a dynamic mix of personal and professional values. Both will influence the interaction.

Monitoring Job Performance, Imparting Knowledge and Skills, and Providing Emotional Support

Social work supervision is ultimately for the benefit of clients, although the recipients of supervision are frontline social workers. From the review of the historical development of social work supervision over the last 120 years in Chapter 1, it can be seen that the root of social work is administrative accountability. This trend became dominant at the end of the twentieth century due to the increasing influence of managerialism. Social work supervision is also in-service training for frontline social workers in human service organizations. To ensure that the supervisee has the motivation and morale to do the job effectively, the supervisor also provides emotional support during the supervisory process. This last function is the unique feature of social work supervision; it differentiates supervision of social workers from supervision of other helping professionals.

Long-term Objectives and Short-term Objectives

As Kadushin and Harkness (2002) observed, the long-term objective of social work supervision is to provide an effective and efficient service to clients. Supervisors, therefore, have to coordinate workers' activities, educate workers so that they can perform their jobs more skillfully, and support workers in their efforts to get the job done. In the short run, the aim of supervision is to improve the workers' professional capacity to do the job effectively, to provide a good context for work, and to help workers feel good about the job.

The Involvement of Four Parties: The Agency, the Supervisor, the Supervisee, and the Client

As Tsui and Ho (1997) noted, the supervisory process does not involve only the supervisor and the supervisee. Four parties—the client, the supervisee, the supervisor, and the agency—participate in the process. This four-part interaction underlines the fact that the client plays a crucial role in the supervisory relationship. Supervision is mainly an indirect method of achieving administrative accountability.

Rich (1993) examined all the existing models of social work supervision, psychotherapy supervision, and clinical supervision. He identified six major features: facilitative environment, supervisory relationship, structural elements, supervisory skills, provision of learning experiences, and supervisory roles. For each feature, Rich (1993) further identified various elements and described them briefly. As noted in Chapter 2, Rich's (1993) summary is a "rich," self-explanatory and practice-specific guide for supervisors. It is also a user-friendly guide for frontline practitioners.

Bruce and Austin (2000) analyzed seven major textbooks on social work supervision: *Supervision in Social Work* (Kadushin, 1992a), *Supervisory Management for the Human Services* (Austin, 1981), *Competent Supervision: Making Imaginative Judgements* (Middleman & Rhodes, 1985), *Supervision and Performance: Managing Professional Work in Human Service Organizations* (Bunker & Wijnberg, 1988), *Interactional Supervision* (Shulman, 1993), *Supervising in the Human Services: The Politics of Practice* (Holloway & Brager, 1989), and *Clinical Social Work Supervision* (Munson, 1993). Bruce and Austin (2000) used Kadushin's (1992a) three functions of social work supervision (i.e., supportive, educational, and administrative) as the basis of classification for the other six books. Munson (1993) emphasized the supportive function, while Shulman's (1993) focus was split between the supportive and educational functions. Bunker and Wijnberg (1988) stressed the educational function, and Austin (1981), the administrative. Holloway and Brager (1989) concentrated on the administrative and educational functions. Bruce and Austin (2000) pointed out that the core supervisory roles suggested by Middleman and Rhodes (1985) can illuminate three functions of supervision: integrative functions, service delivery functions, and linkage functions. The integrative functions of the supervisor involve humanizing the supervisory process, managing tension, and translating ideas into actions. The service delivery functions of the supervisor include teaching the supervisees, socializing the supervisees' career, and evaluating job performance. The linkage functions of the supervisor consist of administering tasks related to service goals, advocating on behalf of supervisees, and making changes that will improve service for better quality (Middleman & Rhodes, 1985).

After reviewing the existing models of supervision, I have designed the model shown in Figure 3.1.

THE SUPERVISORY RELATIONSHIP

The supervisory relationship is the core of social work supervision (Fox, 1983, 1989; Kaiser, 1997). Unfortunately, it has been narrowly defined as a supervisor-supervisee relationship, with no attention to

Figure 3.1 A Comprehensive Model of Social Work Supervision

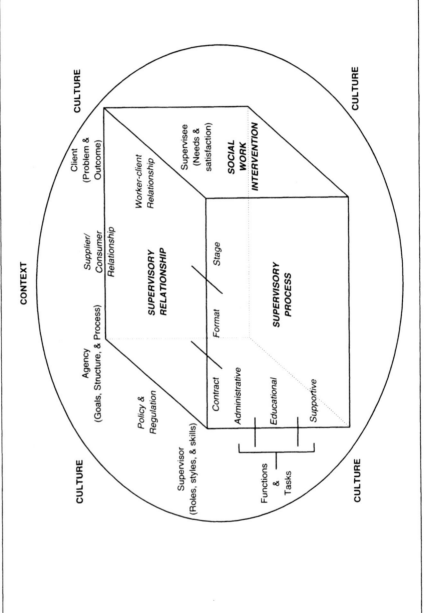

context. This oversimplified view severely limits the scope of meaningful discussion and analysis of the topic. The view fails, for example, to offer any explanation of the fact that the root of social work supervision is administrative, and it neglects the ultimate and most important objective of social work practice—quality of service to clients. This limited perspective on the supervisory relationship has also led researchers to focus exclusively on debates related to the dynamic between the supervisor and the supervisee, such as the compatibility of different supervisory functions and the professional autonomy of frontline social workers. In order to discuss social work supervision in a holistic manner, we must reconceptualize the supervisory relationship as a multifaceted relationship involving the agency, the supervisor, the supervisee, and the client, within a cultural context (see Figure 3.1).

The Agency, the Supervisor, the Supervisee, and the Client

The process of social work supervision in an agency is affected by the agency's organizational goals, organizational structure, policy and procedures, service setting, and organizational climate. All are related to the culture of the task environment of the organization (Glisson, 1985; Kast & Rosenzweig, 1985). As far as the agency is concerned, supervision is a tool used to achieve organizational objectives; it adopts organizational policy and procedures in a specific service setting and within an organizational structure, which is, in turn, part of a specific organizational climate. The supervisor, as a "middle person," is a mediator and a liaison between the agency and the supervisee. On the one hand, supervisors are administrators and, as such, members of the agency's management; on the other hand, they are the most senior frontline staff. Supervisors have to play various roles in order to fulfill their responsibilities. They must follow the agency's policies and procedures and interpret them for their supervisees. During this process, supervisors must make the policies and procedures specific, concrete, and workable. At the same time, supervisors need to pay attention to the morale and job satisfaction of the staff. Supervisees have their own training background, working experience, training needs, and level of competence. All these culturally influenced variables will affect the format and frequency of their supervision. Finally, clients have their own problems. The way in which clients perceive their problems is very much affected by their culture (Chau, 1995; Lee, 1996) and also influences their means of seeking help and using the resources provided by the social workers. Naturally, the outcomes of social work intervention are closely related to culturally embedded conceptions of the worker-client relationship.

The Agency and the Supervisor

Agency policy governs the behavior of supervisors. In some human service organizations, there are well-established policies and accountability systems, which require supervisors to report the progress and outcomes of service delivery to top management. In other organizations, there may not be explicit guidelines. However, the supervisor still serves as a "middle person" in the organization, and he or she is a channel between the agency and the supervisee. The supervisor's monitoring ensures that the supervisee's practice conforms to agency goals. At the same time, the supervisee obtains direction from the supervisor. Thus, the administrative accountability of the supervisee to the agency is established indirectly through supervision. In this sense, the supervisor is primarily a middle-level human service manager.

THE SUPERVISORY PROCESS: THE INTERACTION BETWEEN THE SUPERVISOR AND THE SUPERVISEE

As noted, research on supervision has traditionally focused on the supervisory process. This process is based on the supervisory relationship between the supervisor and the supervisee, which consists of three major components: the supervisory contract, the choice of an appropriate format for supervision, and a process of development. The supervisory contract sets goals, expectations, and tasks. By establishing an agreed-upon contract, the supervisor and the supervisee come to understand their rights and responsibilities. The contract determines their schedule of meetings and specifies the skills required for the job. A supervisory contract can serve as a plan, an agreement, and a standard for evaluation. The format of supervision is determined by several factors: the level of professional autonomy allowed by the agency, the styles and skills of the supervisor, and the needs and experience of the supervisee. Once again, most of these factors are influenced by culture. At various stages in the supervisory process, there are indicators of the progress of both the supervisory relationship and the supervisee's skills. These indicators give the supervisor and the supervisee an opportunity to develop a clear step-by-step action guideline to improve job performance (Tsui, 1998a).

The supervisor-supervisee relationship may also be perceived as a relationship with administrative, professional, and psychological components. For each component, supervisors must fulfill a number of supervisory tasks, and, therefore, they must assume a range of roles. This interactional process is characterized by the use of authority, an exchange of information, and expressions of emotion. These three kinds of interpersonal transactions, in fact, represent the three major supervisory functions—the administrative, educational, and supportive functions—which, of course, overlap.

The Supervisee and the Client

Between the supervisee and the client, there is a worker-client relationship, as well as a professional helping relationship. It is governed by a professional code of ethics and by agency policy. In this worker-client relationship, supervisees use the knowledge they have acquired from their professional training and follow the advice given by their supervisors to achieve the intervention objectives. Possible client outcomes can be a change in relationships, an enhancement of awareness, or a behavioral change. Effective client outcomes are, of course, the ultimate objective of social work supervision. In other words, supervision eventually works for the clients, not only for the workers.

The Client and the Agency

The relationship between the client and the agency can be viewed as a relationship between service consumer and service provider. In the social work field, most service consumers do not have to pay for the service received, except in the case of private practice. The client is not a direct service consumer because the consumer who receives the service and the funding body that pays for it are two separate entities. As long as the government or a donor pays the bill for human services, the agency will not be directly accountable to the client in a real sense. This is also true in the case of a third-party payment arrangement, which is very common in medical care and related insurance programs.

However, as a service consumer, the client is empowered to give feedback to the funding body and, thus, indirectly bring pressure to bear upon the agency.

CULTURE AS THE CONTEXT FOR SUPERVISION

Traditionally, social work supervision has been recognized as an indirect social work practice embedded in an organizational setting (Austin, 1981; Holloway & Brager, 1989; Miller, 1987; Munson, 1993). For this reason, the organization has been taken as the context for supervisory practice, and researchers have focused their studies on the supervisor-supervisee relationship within human service organizations. Hence, investigations in the past have focused on factors relating to this supervisor-supervisee relationship within an organizational context, for example, the use of supervisory authority, the supervisory contract, supervisory roles and styles, and supervisory functions and tasks.

The traditional view, however, is valid only when one perceives supervision as a process involving two parties—the supervisor and the supervisee—both of whom are employees of a human service organization. If one maintains that supervision is an interactional process involving four parties—the agency, the supervisor, the supervisee, and the client—the agency becomes an integral part of the supervision process (Holloway & Brager, 1989). The agency itself is no longer the context for social work supervision. Obviously, if we perceive supervision as a multifaceted interactional process that involves the agency as one of the participating parties, we need to identify the factors that affect all four participating parties. A wider perspective is needed to explain the dynamics of these four parties, a perspective that includes the environment of the organization.

As an enabling process, social work supervision involves considerable interaction and exchange among the agency, the supervisor, the supervisee, and the client, and each of these parties has objectives that are embedded in a specific cultural context. Within this four-party relationship, frontline social workers report the results of their professional intervention to their supervisors. Supervisors report key information about service delivery to the top management of the agency. The agency must be accountable and responsive to the needs of the clients in order to receive the support of the community. Culture deeply influences the problems of clients, the solutions to these problems, the intervention approach of the supervisee, the roles and styles of the supervisors, and the organizational goals and processes of the agency.

Unfortunately, "culture" is easy to discuss but difficult to define. It is an abstract concept and has different meanings for different people in different contexts (Berry & Laponce, 1994; Ingold, 1994). Culture is a shared system of concepts or mental representations, established by convention and reproduced by transmission. Anthropologists in the past have adapted the notion of culture to suit the dominant concerns of the day, and they will continue to do so. Therefore, debates on the correct meaning of culture are always inconclusive (Ingold, 1994). We have to understand that, unless we identify culture as a set of specific traits, it is very difficult to have a meaningful discussion.

The term "culture" was first used by Tylor (1871) to refer to a complex whole that includes knowledge, belief, art, morals, laws, customs, and other capabilities and habits acquired by a member of society. A comprehensive survey by Kroeber and Kluckhohn (1952) identified over 200 formal definitions. They classified these definitions into six groups: descriptive (listing features), historical (emphasizing heritage and descent), normative (emphasizing shared rules), psychological (emphasizing the processes of adaptation and learning), structural (emphasizing organization and pattern), and genetic (emphasizing the origin or genesis of culture). However, no single definition has gained general acceptance (Berry & Laponce, 1994; Goodenough, 1996).

Other scholars have attempted to define "culture" using a fourfold typology (Ingold, 1994; Jenks, 1993). First, culture is a general state of mind; it refers to the aspiration to achieve individual human goals or emancipation. This reflects a highly individualistic philosophical commitment to particularity, difference, and perfection. Second, culture is an embodied collective category. It refers to a state of intellectual and moral development in a society. Culture, in this respect, is the same as civilization. Third, culture is a descriptive and concrete category. It can be conceptualized as the collective body of artistic and intellectual work in a society. This is one of the ways "culture" is used in everyday language. Fourth, culture is a social category—the whole way of life of a people. This is the pluralist and potentially democratic sense of culture often used in sociology, anthropology, and cultural studies (Jenks, 1993).

Greetz (1973) defined "culture" as a historically transmitted pattern of meanings embodied in symbols. For LeVine (1984), it is "a shared organisation of ideas that includes the intellectual, moral, and aesthetic standards prevalent in a community and the meanings of communicative actions. But formal definitions do little to clarify the nature of culture; clarification is only possible through ethnography" (LeVine, 1984, p. 67).

Instead of defining culture, D'Andrade (1984) identified three major views on its nature. One is the notion of culture as knowledge, as the accumulation of information. According to this view, culture can and does accumulate and does not need to be shared if the distribution of knowledge is such that the proper "linking understandings" are maintained. The second view is that culture consists of "conceptual structures" that create the central reality of a people, so that they "inhabit the world they imagine" (Greetz, 1973). According to this view, culture is not just shared, it is intersubjectively shared, so that everyone assumes that others see the same things they see. Culture does not accumulate any more than the grammar of a language accumulates, and the total size of a culture, in terms of its body of information, is relatively small. The entire system appears to be tightly interrelated but not necessarily without contradictions. The third view on the nature of culture mediates between the "culture as knowledge" and the "culture as constructed reality" positions. It views culture and society as entities made up of institutions such as the family, the market, the farm, the church, the village, and so on (D'Andrade, 1984).

Although culture is difficult to define, it is easy to distinguish and identify. It is the way of life and the way of viewing the world of a specific social group. Distinct cultural traits can be identified. Within the context of supervision, culture affects all four parties involved in the supervisory relationship. Social work supervision is a part of a complex theoretical and professional value system and a service network situated inside a particular culture. Therefore, it can only be understood as part of the cultural context of the participants. The objectives and policies of an agency, for example, are shaped by the culture of its top management, the culture of its funding sources, the culture of the community, and the culture of the profession. Supervisory roles, styles, and skills are all very much influenced by the culture of individual supervisors. Similarly, the supervisees' working experience, training needs, and emotional needs are all influenced by their culture. Finally, culture determines how clients interpret their problems and how they get the help necessary to solve them (Chau, 1995; Lee, 1996; Peterson, 1991; Tsang & George, 1998). Thus, all four parties are embedded in a culture, which is the major context for supervision. The emphasis on reciprocity and the family network in Chinese culture, for example, has an explicit and implicit impact on the behavior of the supervisor, the supervisee, the agency, and the client.

However, the notion of culture as the major context for supervision has not received the attention it deserves. In fact, it has largely been neglected by both supervisors and researchers. Little empirical research has been done in this area (Tsui, 1997b). Although there has been a dramatic increase in the literature on cross-cultural social work practice in North America in recent years (Chau, 1995; Kim, 1995; Lee, 1996; Peterson, 1991; Tsang and George, 1998), the important question of how to practice supervision in a specific culture or in a multicultural setting has not been addressed in any of the published empirical literature.

IMPLICATIONS FOR SOCIAL WORK SUPERVISION

Seeing the supervisory relationship as involving four parties helps to explain the behavior of those parties in a more precise way. In the supervisory process, supervisees have to be accountable to the client, but not directly. They are only accountable to the client through the supervisor and the agency. Hence, as long as the social worker is not employed directly by the client, some sort of supervision will probably be necessary.

This perspective also reveals why supervision in private practice has different features. Because the client pays the bill for service, direct service provider-customer accountability is established. The need for indirect accountability through supervision is, therefore, reduced. Of course, third-party payment by various insurance programs may weaken this direct accountability.

The model of social work supervision proposed here provides a holistic view of the context of social work supervision (see Figure 3.1). The culture, not the organization, is recognized as the major context. In addition, the components of social work supervision are reconceptualized within a wider perspective. In this model, the effectiveness of supervision depends on several factors: the relationships among the individual parties (the agency, the supervisor, the supervisee, and the client); the contract, format, and development stages of the supervisory process; the balance among the various supervisory functions; and the relationship between the features of supervision and the culture of the external environment.

This new model of social work supervision shows that past research on supervision confined itself to a narrow perspective: a supervisory process in which the supervisor-supervisee relationship is the focus. Confining attention to the supervisory process has narrowed our vision and limited our discussion to strictly conceived issues. This focus does not contribute significantly to theory building, nor does it provide philosophical insights for scholars or practical action guidelines for practitioners. It is time for us to practice supervision with a wider and wiser perspective.

4

The Contexts
of Supervision

The context of social work supervision refers to the environment—
physical, interpersonal, cultural, and psychological—in which the
session of social work supervision occurs. A thorough understanding
of the context will help us make our supervisory practice more
sensitive, effective, and comfortable. The physical context refers to
the venue, seating arrangement, and atmosphere of the place where the
supervision session is held. The interpersonal context refers to the
dynamic between the supervisor and the supervisee. The cultural context refers to the norms and values of the society in which the supervisor and the supervisee live and work. Finally, the psychological context
concerns the attitudes, emotions, and mentality that the supervisor and
supervisee bring to their sessions, and is a result of their background,
past experience, and personality.

Eisikovitz and his colleagues (1985) studied 63 frontline social
workers in public social service agencies in northern Israel. Two sets of
measurements were used: one to assess the work and treatment environment, and the other to evaluate the quality of professional supervision. It was found that supervisory variables (for example, the
professional development of workers and the administrative skills of
supervisors) were positively correlated with work environment variables (for example, task orientation, independence, and involvement)

and with treatment environment variables (for example, autonomy, spontaneity, and clarity of rules). Based on these findings, Eisikovitz and his colleagues (1985) suggested creating a work context for effective service delivery and integrating all aspects of supervision in the agency policy and training programs for supervisors.

Scott (1965) studied all the social workers in a public social work agency in a small American city. Ninety caseworkers returned self-administered questionnaires and 11 supervisors were interviewed. It was found that the social workers generally accepted the supervision context in their organization, although professionally oriented staff were more critical of the system than those who were not professionally oriented. At the same time, the staff supervised by professionally oriented supervisors were less critical of the supervision system than were the staff under the supervision of less professionally oriented supervisors (Scott, 1965). This finding suggests that the professional frontline staff have higher expectations for supervision, and that professional supervisors provide supervision leading to a higher level of staff satisfaction.

THE PHYSICAL CONTEXT

Human beings are social animals, and, like other animals, they care very much about the space they possess and boundaries in which they live. In social work supervision, the social meaning of the location is more significant than the physical setting itself. One reason for this is that supervisors (and their supervisees) perceive the supervisory relationship as a formal relationship between an employer and employee within a professional organization. The supervision session is usually held in the supervisor's office. This may be due to habit, convenience, or a lack of office space. Still, this arrangement does, to a certain extent, reflect the attitude of supervisors (and, sometimes, their supervisees) and the nature of their interpersonal relationship. As a frontline social worker observed, the fact that the supervision session is in her supervisor's office reminds her that she is a subordinate. Discussions of professional intervention do not take place on an equal footing. Supervisors are also aware of this disparity of status. The supervisor of a youth center observed, "We have a supervision room; I feel like a supervisor. The feeling is so strong that my awareness of being a supervisor is greater." A senior supervisor of a resident rehabilitation network described his feelings: "When we have a supervision session in my office, I am the boss. Whenever we are in the group room, we become more equal."

In fact, the physical setting of the supervision session does affect the atmosphere of the discussion. When the supervision session is held in an interview room, the arrangement safeguards privacy and guarantees concentration, because there are no intrusions and telephone interruptions. However, some supervisees feel as if they are case clients in that venue. As a caseworker for a family service center commented, "When I meet my supervisor in an interview room, she becomes the caseworker and I become a client. She is ready to listen and help, while I am prepared to receive help."

Some supervisors suggest going out for supervision sessions, perhaps to a garden or a coffee shop. This arrangement clearly encourages a more casual attitude, and supervisees often find it easier to express their feelings. Of course, the confidentiality of the discussion must be safeguarded; otherwise, it would be in violation of the profession's code of ethics. Frontline social workers prefer these casual settings; the comfortable and open location enhances relaxed discussion between the supervisor and the supervisee and encourages them to converse as professional peers. As a youth worker told me, "Most of the time, we chose places outside our offices for supervision sessions. It may be a restaurant, a garden, or a university campus. We have tea and snacks. The feeling is relaxed. There are no disturbances, no documents, and no need to remember the work. It is easier to concentrate. In addition, it seems like the relationship between the team leader and me is friendlier. This is because it is very difficult for him to give harsh instructions in such a casual and relaxed atmosphere."

Although frontline social workers say that they prefer open physical settings, this does not mean that supervisors should confine themselves to this kind of arrangement. A variety of physical settings, depending on context, is recommended. If supervisors are giving instructions or conveying official information, their office is a traditional and appropriate place to do so. On occasions when supervisors wish to give emotional support and allow their supervisees to express their feelings, an interview room may be a good choice. If brainstorming or creative thinking is required, an open space with more physical freedom could be inspiring. Of course, no matter where you are, privacy, confidentiality, convenience, and comfort should be taken into account. Most important, the setting should be acceptable to the supervisee. The basic principle underlying the choice of physical setting is to make the supervisee feel secure and comfortable.

The seating arrangement also plays an important role, although it is often neglected by the supervisor. The supervisee is a professional social worker, and the supervision session is an opportunity to talk to the supervisor directly. The session is itself an intensive and focused discussion. However, for supervisors, it is just one part of the routine, because the supervisor is in charge of a team of professional staff. The sensitivity of the supervisor is naturally lower than that of the supervisee. However, a busy schedule is not an excuse, and the importance of the seating arrangement should not be underestimated.

There are three common seating arrangements. The face-to-face discussion across an office desk denotes the most formal relationship within a hierarchy in a bureaucracy. Naturally, the discussion will tend to be related to administrative issues such as the effectiveness of the intervention, the efficiency of the service delivery, and even the submission of service statistics reports and other paperwork. This seating arrangement enables the supervisor to instruct the supervisee and discuss job performance face to face, with direct eye contact. Supervisees, whether they like it or not, must respond and be held accountable. However, both parties may find it troublesome to refer to documents and notes. In addition, it is difficult to have physical contact (with the exception of an opening handshake). The arrangement does not encourage a sense of a united purpose; instead, the supervisee is forced to face the supervisor. Supervisees may not feel comfortable expressing their feelings in this setting unless the feeling is very strong or they are very assertive. In sum, the face-to-face seating arrangement is only appropriate for task-oriented, instructional, and administrative briefings and reporting. It forces the staff to "face" the boss, that is, to face reality.

The second common seating arrangement is one in which the supervisee sits next to the supervisor at a 90-degree angle. This is the seating arrangement used during clinical encounters such as between a counselor and client or a medical consultation. In this position, the physical distance between the supervisor and the supervisee is reduced. Both supervisors and supervisees may find it easier to express their feelings, particularly because their nonverbal clues are more visible. However, this clinically oriented arrangement may encourage the supervisee to feel like a client. There are supervisors who tend to play the role of therapist during the supervision session, but some supervisees are uncomfortable with this dynamic, because it appears to diminish their status as professional practitioners. In addition, discussions of personal matters in professional settings blur the boundary between personal life and professional practice. Without the consent and invitation of their supervisees, supervisors should not give advice regarding personal issues. Even when they are invited to discuss these issues, supervisors should view supervisees as colleagues and remain aware of the necessity of differentiating personal and professional matters. Supervisors must bear in mind the sensitivity of personal issues. Otherwise, both the privacy of the staff and the mechanism of professional practice will be threatened.

In the third seating arrangement, the supervisor and the supervisee sit side by side. Of course, this seating arrangement cannot be easily arranged in a small office. Sometimes, a group room or conference room is used. Even in an office, it can be managed with some foresight; a sofa, for example, would allow both parties to sit side by side comfortably. This seating arrangement carries a symbolic message of friendliness and equality between the supervisor and the supervisee. Their physical separation is minimal. Each party can easily see the facial expression of the other. It is also easy for each to read the documents in the other's hand. Inhibitions are reduced to a minimum and mutual trust is enhanced. It is easy to have physical contact when it is necessary and appropriate. Of course, any such physical contact must be politically correct and culturally acceptable. Although the use of this informal seating arrangement can help to build relationships and facilitate communication and a sense of partnership between the supervisor and the supervisee, it may not be suitable for every situation. For example, when the supervisor is required to impose a disciplinary action or assert supervisory authority, this seating arrangement would be inappropriate.

In fact, there is no perfect seating arrangement that suits every kind of supervision situation. It is best to consider the context and agree upon an arrangement before conducting the session. On the basis of my observation of supervisory practice, it seems most supervisors use a mix of seating arrangements. The top priority is to ensure both parties feel respected and secure.

THE INTERPERSONAL CONTEXT

Relationships are the most important medium in which social work intervention occurs. As an enabling social work process, supervision is embedded in the relationship between the supervisor and the supervisee. Both have three roles. First, they are people with unique personalities. Second, they are social workers who have professional values, knowledge, and skills. Third, they are employees (usually of different rank) of the same human service organization.

No matter what role they play, the supervisor and the supervisee interact with each other as human beings and their relationship is the context for their interpersonal communication. This relationship is a precondition of mutual trust and communication, and also of effective teamwork. Consequently, the supervisor should try to be sincere, warm, friendly, and open. The best course of action is simply to say what you believe. You should not create an obliging impression when you do not intend to follow through. Be a genuine person and a humane social worker, and then you can be a good supervisor. Start by determining who your staff are, not what they should do.

In the context of supervision, there is the potential for three kinds of relationships. First, the supervisor may treat the supervisee as a subordinate in the organization. In this situation, the supervision will tend to be administratively oriented. Giving instructions and monitoring job performance will become the focus. This formal and hierarchical relationship will cease automatically as soon as the supervisee leaves the human service organization. Second, the supervisor may treat the supervisee as a professional peer. In this case, supervision will be professionally oriented. Enhancing professional growth in terms of values, knowledge, and skills will be the focus of social work supervision. The relationship between peers is longer lasting and may extend throughout the professional careers of the supervisor and the supervisee. Third, the supervisor and the supervisee may view their relationship as a friendship. Each perceives the other as a friend, as well as a colleague. If this is the case, the supervision will be more supportive. Personal concerns, shared feelings, and mutual support will be expressed in supervision sessions and in the daily encounters between the supervisor and the supervisee. Such a relationship could last a lifetime. Family members of the supervisor and the supervisee may also become good friends. From my experience, many social work supervisors and frontline staff maintain long-lasting friendships after they leave the workplace. Still, as Atherton (1986) observed, supervision is a work-related activity, which focuses on the benefit of clients. As long as they deal with their clients successfully, the supervisor and the supervisee are not obliged to develop a personal relationship. Social workers are also human beings. Personal friendship develops gradually and naturally from daily teamwork. In my view, it is more important to locate the boundary between a professional relationship and a personal relationship than to pretend that there is no such thing as a personal relationship in the supervisory process. In human service organizations, some guidelines or, at least, a consensus should be worked out in order to achieve a clear outline of the boundaries of the supervisory relationship.

Brown and Bourne (1996) distinguished 10 common issues in the supervisory relationship, which will help us to understand the problems that may occur. The first potentially problematic situation arises when a new supervisor takes over an established team. The supervisor may lack the necessary confidence and knowledge, and may feel compelled to demonstrate his or her professional competence immediately. The supervisor will not be familiar with the daily work routine of the service unit and the subculture of the staff team. Demonstrations of supervisory authority without a comprehensive understanding of the context may easily undermine staff morale and hinder the development of a team with a high level of motivation. At the same time, such demonstrations may provoke rebellious behavior on the part of the frontline staff. For example, a newly appointed supervisor of a family service center tried to assert his authority on his first day on the job. He asked the staff to relocate the plants in the reception area. He tripped over one of the plants when he came to work the next day. None of the staff warned him that the plant was in an unsuitable location because they were not happy with his authoritative instructions.

Second, the supervisor and the supervisee may have a complicated personal and professional relationship. For example, if personal friends were to enter into a supervisory relationship, it would be very difficult to differentiate the formal relationship from the informal relationship. Whenever two relationships are confused, there is inter-role conflict. The resolution of such difficulties depends on the wisdom and experience of both the supervisor and the supervisee. One of the ways to deal with conflicting roles is to set a clear mutually agreed upon boundary. The human service organization may have guidelines to help staff members differentiate the two kinds of relationships. For example, different time periods may be used to set boundaries: the supervisory relationship is maintained during office hours, and friendship resumes after work. As a youth worker told me, "Although I am the classmate of my supervisor, as a supervisee, I always remind myself that she is my supervisor during the office hours. She becomes my old classmate again at alumni reunions."

The third issue arises from gender and race. The relationship between a supervisor and a supervisee of different genders or races can be very tense. Their orientations may be very different. It takes time, patience, and wisdom to establish mutual understanding. The best course of action is to respect the other person's point of view. The handling of gender and race issues in social work supervision will be discussed in subsequent sections on cross-gender and cross-cultural supervision.

Fourth, there may be an ideological conflict between the supervisor and the supervisee. If there is a difference in political beliefs, the office may become a political forum. Usually, supervisors are more conservative than frontline social workers because of the difference in age, socio-economic status, and position in the hierarchy. Of course, there are exceptions. If the human service organization has a particular ideological commitment, it should be stated explicitly in writing in the recruitment process and clearly explained in the orientation period. If not, it may be better for staff to view their own ideological commitment as a guide for personal behavior rather than professional practice. Otherwise, the supervisory process may become an endless political debate. All parties involved in the supervisory process—the supervisor, the supervisee, the organization, and the client—will suffer.

The fifth complication occurs when there is transference on the part of the supervisee. Transference is the unconscious replaying of a past dynamic within a current relationship. In the supervisory situation, the supervisee uses the supervisor as a substitute for somebody else. This emotional reaction to the supervisor will hinder the professional development of the supervisee; the relationship will be distorted by personal and emotional complexities. If this kind of psychological transference occurs, it is better to address it immediately and frankly. For example, I had a supervisee who jotted down everything I said to her. I was disturbed by her behavior; it seemed that she did not believe what I said. When I pointed this out in a friendly manner, she told me that she had been misled by a former supervisor in another organization. Then I understood that her behavior was a reasonable, self-protective response arising from a bad experience in a previous work environment. I told her to talk to other social workers about my trustworthiness. After a short period of time, she had a greater sense of security and was able to accept my comments at face value. In this situation, it is necessary to achieve mutual acceptance and open communication.

The sixth issue arises because of the parallels between the supervisor-supervisee relationship and the worker-client relationship. Although these two relationships are similar, they should not be confused. The supervisory relationship in social work practice provides emotional support, but its primary concerns are the monitoring of job performance and the development of professional competence. It is a professional relationship between two colleagues with different responsibilities and experiences. The worker-client relationship is by nature a helping relationship. If these two kinds of relationships are confused, the supervisee becomes a client, and the supervisory relationship becomes a therapeutic relationship. The frontline social worker will never grow up.

The seventh complication occurs when personal information is discussed in the supervision session; the boundary between the professional and the personal may become blurred. Once again, the intersection of personal and professional spheres should be handled carefully. It is not advisable to discuss personal issues in supervision sessions even when the supervisor and the supervisee are close. It is very difficult for the supervisor not to be affected by private information about the personal life of individual staff. When personnel decisions are made, this information may become a major consideration and may unfairly affect the prospects of the supervisee or other staff members.

The eighth potentially problematic issue is the sexual orientation of the supervisor or the supervisee. Different sexual orientations should be accepted in an open society; they do not affect job performance. An inclusive policy and an open attitude toward diversity will help resolve this difference. The supervisor, however, needs to remain sensitive in this context. In some cultures, the question of sexual orientation is considered taboo; it cannot even be discussed. Even in an open society, sexual orientation is still a delicate political issue. It has implications for human service delivery, the client's perception of the organization, and the supervisor-supervisee relationship.

The ninth issue occurs when supervisees are unwilling to share their difficulties. Sometimes this is called "no problem supervision." In fact, this kind of supervisory relationship reflects the supervisee's lack of self-confidence, as well as a lack of mutual trust between the supervisor and the supervisee. There is no frank discussion of problems and possible solutions; the supervisee just says everything is fine and discourages further discussion. As a result, there is no meaningful supervision. In this situation, the supervisor should act as a role model and share his or her work-related problems with the supervisee. This open attitude will probably encourage the supervisee to be equally frank. However, the supervisor should understand that it may take some time before the supervisee builds up confidence and feels comfortable expressing genuine feelings in supervision sessions.

Finally, problems arise when a supervisee's behavior does not meet professional standards. In this situation, the supervisor is forced to make difficult decisions and take disciplinary action. It is crucial to use authority wisely and identify possible alternatives.

Most social workers are employees of human service organizations. The organizational context, including the organizational goals, structure, processes, and culture, become the immediate task environment for their professional practice. Organizational goals refer to the vision, mission, and objectives of the human service organization. The structure of a specific organization determines the way in which it divides its workloads, integrates results, and makes its staff members accountable to the various stakeholders. Organizational processes include the ways in which managerial decisions are made, goals are accomplished, and resources are allocated. The culture of an organization reflects its values, rituals, behavior patterns, and atmosphere. All of these characteristics of an organization influence the format and structure of social work supervision. In order for supervision to develop, or even survive, its characteristics must match those of the organization. It was mentioned that certain kinds of service settings are suited to certain formats of supervision. Supervision in a clinical setting is significantly different from that in a team service delivery setting (Erera & Lazar, 1994a). Social work supervision in a medical social work setting is usually case and task oriented. However, social work supervision is less clearly formulated in a small community work team, because the nature of the work is diffuse and autonomous (Kadushin & Harkness, 2002).

THE CULTURAL CONTEXT

Social work supervision is practiced in three overlapping spheres. The innermost circle is the relationship between the supervisor and the supervisee. The second circle is the organizational context. The outer circle is the cultural context of the specific situation in which the supervisor and the supervisee are placed. As noted earlier, social work supervision involves four parties: the supervisee, the supervisor, the agency, and the client. All are members of society. Culture is an abstract concept that is based on the guidelines for social behavior of members of a society; it is a product of social action and a process that guides the future action of people living within a certain context. Culture determines the way members of a society view the world, make decisions, behave, and evaluate the behavior of others (Goodenough, 1961, 1996). Culture can be defined as a system of shared ideas, concepts, rules, and meanings that exist and are expressed in human life (Keesing, 1981).

Social work supervision is part of a complex theoretical and professional value system; it involves service networks situated in a particular culture. Culture influences all four parties involved in the process of social work supervision. Therefore, social work supervision can only be understood in a particular cultural context; any model of supervision is a product of the cultural context in which it arises. This may be why it is so difficult for a supervisor to oversee staff members who come from a different culture. It may also account for difficulties that arise when a supervisor is paired with a supervisee of a different gender, social class, or educational background.

THE PSYCHOLOGICAL CONTEXT

The psychological context of social work supervision has never been discussed in the literature or explored by researchers. However, the way in which the supervisor and the supervisee perceive the supervisory process has a great impact on the process and its result. These perceptions may not be the result of rational thinking; they may be based on impressions arising from personal history, ideas acquired during practice, or feelings engendered by the internal or external environment. Young supervisors often treat their supervisees as fieldwork students, because that is the treatment they received in their own fieldwork practice. Some supervisees (and some supervisors) perceive close supervision as a mechanism for monitoring unmotivated staff whose job performance is unsatisfactory. Supervisees may feel insecure in supervision sessions because the unemployment rate in the field is high. Whatever the perspectives of the supervisor and the supervisee are, the supervision will tend to resemble them. This is because psychological state is also a context in which supervisory practice is embedded. The supervisor and the supervisee should, therefore, try to make the supervisory process a pleasant experience, which allows for the development of trust and learning.

Kaiser (1997) pointed out that the most important element in the supervisory relationship is "shared meaning." This refers to the mutual understanding and agreement between the supervisor and the supervisee. The more shared meaning, the more effective the supervision will be. Clear communication is necessary to reduce differences and develop shared meaning. For example, in cases of cross-gender or cross-cultural supervision, there are so many differences in terms of traits, norms, and interpretations so that shared meaning is difficult to establish. A clearly stated supervisory contract may help to establish shared meaning. However, the attitudes of both the supervisor and the supervisee are also important. For example, it may not be possible to achieve a genuine consensus among staff members regarding necessary budget cuts even when there is a clearly stated formal supervisory contract. Staff may accept opinions without fully endorsing them. The approach to intervention is the core of shared meaning because the ultimate goal of supervision is to serve the clients effectively and efficiently. According to Kaiser (1997), four major components must be addressed: the approach to intervention, the ways people change, the role of practitioner, and the definition of healthy behavior.

Trust is the most important element of the psychological context of supervision. It encompasses respect and a sense of security (Kadushin & Harkness, 2002; Kaiser, 1997; Munson, 2002; Shulman, 1993). As Kaiser (1997) observed, respect can be interpreted as demonstration of the supervisor's esteem for the supervisee. A sense of security is evident when a supervisee feels free to take risks without fearing the supervisor's criticism. As Loganbill, Hardy, and Delworth (1982) pointed out, the common dilemma in supervision is the potential conflict between growth-promoting and accountability-maintaining functions. The growth-promoting functions require a trusting relationship between the supervisor and the supervisee. However, this trust may be threatened by the necessity to be accountable to top management or funding agencies. Some supervisors and supervisees may be tempted to cover up their mistakes instead of addressing them with their supervisors.

A HOLISTIC CONTEXT FOR SUPERVISION

Social work supervision can and should be viewed from a holistic perspective. It is practiced in a multifaceted context. It is an intensive, interactional, and interpersonal process involving two professional parties who are accountable to the agency and the client. Taking a large view, the physical, interpersonal, cultural, and psychological contexts will greatly influence the format, structure, content, and even the results of social work supervision. This is why both parties should be contextually sensitive, personally sincere, and psychologically pleasant. The success of supervision sessions depends on physical comfort, a harmonious relationship, organizational appropriateness, psychological well-being, and cultural sensitivity.

5

Administrative Functions

M ost social workers practice in a bureaucratic setting. According to Kadushin and Harkness (2002), bureaucracy has six features. First, it depends on the specialization of functions and tasks, with a high level of division of labor. Second, it creates a hierarchy of authority. Third, staff members exercise authority based on their position. Fourth, people are recruited, selected, and assigned to positions in the organization on the basis of objective, technical qualifications. Fifth, there are rules and procedures applied to all staff members. Finally, all organizational activities are deliberately and rationally planned to achieve the organization's objectives.

In human service organizations, supervisors are the most senior frontline practitioners and the most junior members of the management. They experience three kinds of constraints (Perlmutter, 1990). There are professional constraints due to their status as members of the social work profession (Johnson, 1972; Yan & Tsui, 2003). They cannot discredit the values, knowledge, and skills of the social work profession, which are expressed clearly in its professional code of ethics. There are organizational constraints based on the organization's goals and structure and the expectations of the top management and its executives. Then there are the constraints that supervisors experience as a result of race, gender, age, personality, time management, the transition from frontline to management, and the potential for burnout

(Perlmutter, 1990). All these constraints contribute to stress and may make the supervisor's job a complicated and difficult one. Supervisors become marginalized in the organization, although they are part of the management. They feel lonely, despite their position as leaders of a team, because they do not actively participate in the frontline service. They feel insecure, even though they have authority to monitor and influence frontline social workers.

Melichercik (1984) conducted an in-depth study of supervisors. He used the diary method for data collection. A nonrandom sample of 85 social work supervisors from 12 social welfare agencies in Ontario were sent logs to record their daily activities for one week. This study provided a clear picture of the practice of social work supervision in Ontario. Supervisors spent the largest portion of their time fulfilling the administrative duties of program management. Educational activities also occupied a large portion of the supervisors' time. These activities could be divided into two categories. The first was teaching ways to deal with procedures, policies, guidelines, and standards, and the second focused on staff development and the enhancement of skill competence. While an important study, the report provides a picture of, but not a practice guide for, supervision.

Poertner and Rapp (1983) used task analysis to construct a description of social work supervisors' daily activities. All the social work supervisors ($N = 120$), one-third of the supervisees ($N = 227$), and 22 fieldwork supervisors of a large child welfare agency in Illinois were invited to rank the importance of a list of tasks. The study indicated that, according to the population studied, the dominant function of supervision is the administrative function, including staff, caseload, and organizational management. Greenspan and her colleagues (1991) conducted a survey of 198 supervisees drawn by random sampling. All were experienced social workers. It was found that, despite their experience, they received a significant amount of supervision. Experienced practitioners continue to want clinical supervision, but many feel that its quality is not consistently high. Researchers recommend that advanced supervision should be included as a specialization within social work practice.

In human service organizations, social workers are required to demonstrate job performance, fulfill managerial duties, and satisfy the expectations of various stakeholders. All three functions rely on the provision of supervisory authority.

JOB PERFORMANCE

The major objective of social work supervision is to monitor the job performance of frontline social workers. The task of reaching a clear understanding about job performance is difficult because there are many conflicting views (Landy & Farr, 1990; Leiren, 1990; Ritchie, 1992). There are conflicting views of specific stakeholders (e.g., agencies, staff, clients, and government) who have different expectations, interests, and demands. In addition, there is a wide range of definitions provided by researchers who examine job performance from a number of perspectives and focus on different features. As a result, it is very difficult to define job performance clearly.

Job performance evaluation is the appraisal of the worker's fulfillment of duties during a specified period of time. It is job related and time limited. It focuses on the quality of accomplishments (Kadushin & Harkness, 2002). Job performance evaluation is useful to the worker, the agency, the supervisor, and the client. For workers, job performance evaluations provide a valuable measurement of their achievement, which will help them to attain future professional growth. For the immediate supervisor, job performance evaluation is a golden opportunity to examine what the worker really does. It is the most important source of information for planning staff development programs and assignment exercises. For the agency, job performance evaluation is a mechanism for monitoring output and quality of service, in order to be accountable to the community. For the client, job performance evaluation is an indirect mechanism to control the behavior of the professional social workers, in order to safeguard client's rights.

However, job performance evaluation is easier said than done. The process is vulnerable in at least six areas (Kadushin & Harkness, 2002). First, the halo effect refers to a situation in which one outstanding area dominates all other areas. Second, the leniency effect leads the supervisor to tolerate rather than condemn poor performance. Third, the central tendency encourages supervisors to rate all areas of performance as average or fair. Fourth, the recency effect refers to the tendency of supervisors to give more weight to recent performance because the memory is still fresh. Fifth, contrast error occurs when the supervisor compares the performance of a worker with that of other workers instead of an absolute standard. Sixth, the negativity effect refers to the fact that supervisors always pay more attention to negative performance rather than positive performance.

Job Performance as a Standard

From the viewpoint of the human service organization, job performance can be measured according to objective standards. It is an accomplishment that can be quantified and compared. In general, human service organizations use the quality, quantity, and timeliness of outcomes to assess staff performance (Bernardin, 1984). When job performance is measured against a standard, it is easy for the human service organization to conduct performance appraisals in order to make relevant personnel decisions (Cummings & Schwartz, 1973; Landy & Farr, 1990). According to this view of job performance, work is a set of tasks directed toward an end result. The main purpose of standardizing job performance is to ensure that the staff meet the expectations of their employers, the human service organizations. However, while job performance is an indicator of the staff's ability to perform various functions required by the organization (Henderson, 1984), it is not necessarily a measure of their capacity to fulfill their mission. This goal displacement encourages frontline social workers to focus on the completion of the job rather than pursue the larger aims of their profession. Work becomes simply a means to an end.

Job Performance as a Behavior

Job performance can also be identified with the behavior of the staff (Henderson, 1984; Leiren, 1990). Some supervisors believe that the personality traits of the staff predict their behavior on the job. This is not necessarily true, however. The staff's behavior is determined by a number of factors: personal, professional, organizational, and environmental. In addition, various stakeholders—the agency, the client, the government, and the profession—make demands that affect the behavior of the staff. Unfortunately, these demands are sometimes mutually exclusive. When job performance is viewed as behavior, it becomes something observable—"what has been done by the staff" (Campbell, McHenry, & Wise, 1990). However, not everything done by the staff, especially by professional frontline social workers, can be readily observed. For example, clients may not allow supervisors to observe the intervention process in person. The long-term effect of jobs undertaken by helping professionals is not immediately evident. In addition, some of the jobs in human services, such as counseling and outreach youth work, are outside the sphere of the supervisor's observation.

Job Performance as a Process

Job performance can also be viewed as a process (Leiren, 1990), in which case the focus is on how frontline social workers get the job done. The process consists of those activities that contribute to the final output (Goodman & Fichman, 1983). These activities are an indication of the values, knowledge, and skills of the frontline workers. According to this view, "how" help is given is more important than "what" kind of help is given. The relationship between frontline social workers and clients is an important determinant of job performance. Evaluation is not confined to the end result; it takes into account the stages of the intervention process. This focus on process is particularly relevant to social workers, who cannot fully control the outcome of their service. Their work differs from that of the manufacturing sector, for example, where the final product is more easily controlled.

Job Performance as a Social Construct

In summary, different people perceive job performance in different ways. From a temporal perspective, job performance can be determined immediately after the job has been completed (if job performance is measured according to a standard). Or it can be determined by following all the stages of the intervention (if job performance is considered as a process). The behavioral approach takes into account both past and present behaviors. A comprehensive definition of job performance, however, must take into account three major components: staff performance, organizational performance, and quality of service (see Figure 5.1).

In a human service organization, staff performance is measured against the standard set by the organization's funding sources, and quality of service refers to the process of service delivery. Each of the three components is influenced by certain factors. The expectations of human service organizations influence organizational performance; the personal and professional qualities of the social worker determine staff performance; and the needs of clients affect the type and quality of service. Each component has a dynamic relationship with the others, leading to an exchange of information, power, time, money, and personnel. The interaction of the three components provides a process model for social workers.

Figure 5.1

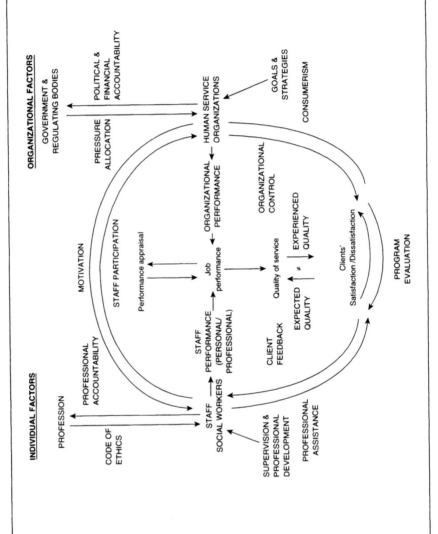

STAFF PERFORMANCE

Staff performance refers to the personal and professional performance of the social worker. Personal performance is the actualization of the personal qualities of individual staff, and it includes hereditary characteristics and talents, along with the traits instilled by upbringing. Professional performance refers to the application of professional values, knowledge, and skills, which are acquired through training programs and exposure to professional practice. Both personal and professional performance contribute to the total performance of a social worker, and during evaluations, personal characteristics, as well as professional skills, are assessed.

Stakeholders place a wide range of demands on the personal and professional performance of the social worker. As individuals, social workers have their own faith, conscience, and life goals, and, to a certain extent, they pursue their personal goals at work. This "inner" accountability influences their decisions and actions. We should not underestimate this commitment to personal ideals. Supervisors should learn the life goals of their staff and align them with the organizational goals. If supervisors wish to motivate their staff to achieve a high level of job performance, they must provide them with the opportunity to actualize their own ideals on the job.

As helping professionals, social workers are, by definition, members of a profession. They must practice social work according to the expectations of a professional association; the behavior of professionals is regulated by a code of ethics. The code is a summary of professional values that reflects both societal values and the interests of the profession. Professional codes of ethics are usually published and are distributed to every member of the profession. The professional association monitors its members to ensure that the code is maintained. The monitoring body possesses a great deal of authority, and members who violate the code may lose their right to practice. This kind of "professional control" ensures that social workers are, to a certain extent, accountable to the professional association.

QUALITY OF SERVICE

For most supervisors, the primary purpose of supervision is to ensure quality of service by providing advice on service direction and by ensuring that the tasks are well performed. Their evaluations take into account not only the end product but also the process itself, which can be monitored by reading case recordings and program progress reports. This monitoring mechanism aims to fulfill the administrative demands of the agency and the funding source. If there are problems in the service operations, the supervisor must work with the supervisees to improve the service.

Mr. Choy, an experienced supervisor of a residential rehabilitation unit, said, "The supervisor has a leading role in keeping the service going. When you find something wrong or when the staff have difficulties in operations, you have to talk to them. It is important to understand the views of the staff through supervision. Is it workable? How? Is there anyone willing to do it?"

Mr. Wong, who is in charge of a counseling center, expressed his view: "The major aim of supervision is to make sure that the staff match the objective of the center, including planning and skills."

In a sense, then, supervision is a mechanism to ensure the output and quality of service. The supervisor should help the staff to understand the public demand for accountability, especially to service users. In order to improve service, supervisors should teach practical working skills. The functions of supervision are not purely administrative. As one supervisor commented, "a supervisor is a supporter, a counselor, and an educator."

Social workers have to give professional advice and assistance to their clients. If the advice and assistance they provide is satisfactory, then the quality of service will very likely be good, as long as other factors are controlled. Clients may provide feedback to social workers, even though the balance of power between social worker and client is not even. This feedback may be positive or negative, and may be given directly or indirectly, explicitly or implicitly. Such responses have an impact on the personal and professional performance of the social worker. Professional assistance and client feedback are both exchanges between social workers and clients, exchanges that represent the dynamic relationship between staff performance and quality of service.

Most social workers are not private practitioners but employees of human service organizations, either governmental or nongovernmental. Their performance is regularly appraised. This administrative monitoring compels social workers to take their supervisors' expectations into consideration. Under these circumstances, the quality of service provided to clients is not a social worker's only concern. Social workers must also take into account their organizational performance (for example, resource acquisition and cost effectiveness) because their career prospects are determined by the results of performance appraisals. The decisions of the top management of human service organizations are based on those appraisals. These decisions to promote, demote, transfer, or recommend have an enormous impact on the social worker's career. This administrative accountability is sometimes more influential than professional accountability.

Harkness and Hensley (1991) conducted an experiment with a supervisor, four social workers, and 161 clients to support their contention that research on supervision should be focused on client outcomes. The experiment assessed the influence of helping skills and relationships, in both supervision and practice, on client outcomes. A social work supervisor gave two male and two female workers supervision for 16 weeks. For the first eight weeks, mixed-focused supervision was used, which emphasizes administration, training, and clinical consultation. For the last eight weeks, client-focused supervision, which emphasizes staff intervention and client outcomes, was provided. When these two types of supervision were compared on the basis of their effect on client satisfaction and general contentment, the results indicated that client-focused supervision is significantly more effective than mixed-focused supervision in achieving client satisfaction with the attainment of goals, help received, and the worker-client partnership. Harkness (1995) replicated the 1991 study, using four social workers from community health centers (two males and two females) and 161 clients as subjects. The study—an examination of the impact of skills and the supervisory relationship on supervised practice—was a test of Shulman's (1993) interactional helping theory. The predicted associations among the skills, relationships, and outcomes of practice were tested by calculating six correlation coefficients between client ratings of the worker-client relationship, worker helpfulness, goal attainment, and generalized contentment. The study indicated that supervisory skills and the supervisory relationship have a significant effect on client outcomes.

ORGANIZATIONAL PERFORMANCE

Patti (1985) defined organizational performance in terms of efficiency, acquisition of resources, staff satisfaction and participation, and service effectiveness. The first three components are aspects of managerial effectiveness. The last, service effectiveness, refers to the attainment of the goals of service, which is usually determined by clients. As Patti (1988) pointed out, service effectiveness takes into account organizational systems, service quality, and client satisfaction. The main issue, however, is not to determine the components of organizational performance but to establish the means to assess it. As Reid (1988) stated, "no matter how it is done, assessment of effectiveness comes down to human judgement" (p. 45).

Most human service organizations depend on public money for their survival. The government, as a funding agency and a regulating body, can exert financial control. However, the government is not the only party that influences the organizational performance of human service organizations. Clients also demand competent quality of service. This demand can be expressed in consumer movements. Empowered clients have organized themselves into consumer groups in order to voice their demands. Clients influence human service organizations by putting pressure on regulating bodies through various political channels (for example, by lobbying politicians or by participating in elections). Of course, human service organizations do exert some control over individual clients. Clients must abide by the rules and regulations set by the organizations. Those who are not ready to do so may find that their right to receive help is jeopardized, or even forfeited.

Human service organizations must also respond to feedback from staff, particularly those organizations with a high level of staff participation or strong trade unions. Staff influence can be exerted in two ways: staff can organize themselves and take collective action, or individual staff members can respond to policies with passive resistance (for example, by adopting a negative attitude toward their job or devoting less effort to it).

Conflicting demands from various constituencies can complicate the operation of human service organizations. Different stakeholders have different conceptions of the goals of the organization. These conceptions are, in turn, dictated by various considerations (Reid, 1988). For example, as Reid (1988) noted, if two services have the same effect, a regulating body will adopt the less expensive alternative. While it is difficult to demonstrate the superiority of one service to another in terms of effectiveness, it is often easy to do so in terms of cost.

Quality of service does not exist independently; it is affected by job performance (Osborne, 1992). The clients' first priority is to acquire the highest quality of service. As Patti (1988) observed, service quality includes accessibility, timeliness, consistency, humane treatment, and technical proficiency.

In principle, the quality of service should be the outcome of job performance; it is the end result of the efforts of human service organizations. It is also the mission of social workers. Clients usually have expectations regarding quality of service, which the actual quality of service may not meet. If the experienced quality is better than the expected quality, the discrepancy is a positive one, and clients feel satisfied. If, however, the discrepancy is a negative one, clients are dissatisfied. When clients are empowered, the level of expected quality of service rises, and clients become more difficult to satisfy.

SUPERVISOR AS MANAGER

Kadushin and Harkness (2002) maintained that social work supervisors must fulfill 11 administrative functions. The first eight functions address the stages of human resource management, from recruiting staff to getting the job done. They are staff recruitment and selection; job induction; work planning; work assignment; work delegation; monitoring, reviewing, and evaluating work; coordinating work; and communication. The other three functions are related to the managerial roles supervisors assume. As an advocate, the supervisor must fight for the rights of the staff. As an administrator, the supervisor must act as a buffer between the top management and the frontline staff. Finally, the supervisor should also act as a change agent for agency policy and community environment.

Munson (2002) noted that, according to Sennett's (1980) study of authority, supervisors should never attempt to direct the work of others if they are not, themselves, proficient in that area. This corroborates Kadushin's findings in the United States (1992b); supervisees do not mind the supervisor's exercise of administrative authority, but they do not like to be taught by supervisors who lack the necessary professional expertise. The issue of authority has received little attention in social work literature (Munson, 1976, 2002; Tsui, 2001).

It was noted that social workers must be accountable to various stakeholders at various levels. At the level of service accountability, social workers must satisfy clients' needs and help solve their problems. As members of the social work profession, social workers are professionally accountable; they must adhere to the code of ethics and regulations set by the professional body. Within the bureaucracy of human service organizations, social workers are financially accountable to funding sources (government and donors). Social workers must adhere to the goals, policies, and regulations of the human service organization, so they are also administratively accountable to the board, which is mainly made up of volunteers from the community. Finally, social workers are politically accountable to various pressure groups. Supervisors act as mediators and ensure that social workers recognize their accountability but are not exploited.

In addition to the range of accountabilities described previously, there is also internal accountability. Social workers are accountable to each other. Frontline social workers are accountable to their senior staff. The senior staff, in turn, are accountable to the junior staff in matters pertaining to administrative policies, personnel management, use of resources, and service policies. In order to fulfill their obligations, supervisors must be fair, consistent, reasonable, and dynamic.

THE TRANSITION FROM FRONTLINE WORKER TO SUPERVISOR

Austin (1981) suggested that new supervisors must ask themselves several questions: Why did I become a supervisor? Why do my former colleagues treat me differently? Why do I feel caught in the middle—between my workers and top management? How do I use the skills acquired in helping clients in my new job of helping workers? Austin (1981) also suggested that new supervisors must learn new methods, which involve changes in the use of authority, decision-making style, relationship orientation, outcome orientation, and colleague orientation.

The Use of Authority: The Shift From Professional to Organizational Authority

As frontline workers, social workers gain authority from their competence, knowledge, and skills. Ideally, supervisors build on this foundation and enhance their supervisees' professional authority. The national survey conducted by Kadushin (1992b) supports this view. Supervisees commented that they had the greatest respect for those supervisors who demonstrated competence, skill, and problem solving. Unfortunately, however, not every supervisor possesses sufficient professional knowledge and skills. In such cases, supervisors often simply assert the power that they have been given by the top management. Kadushin (1992b) found that the supervisor's administrative authority is easily accepted by supervisees. However, it is unwise to rely on administrative authority rather than professional knowledge when teaching frontline workers. Frontline workers do not like administrators who pretend to be teachers. Because supervisory authority is such a sensitive, difficult, and delicate issue, many newly appointed supervisors avoid using their authority even when they need to do so. They know that an effective social work team relies on harmony among team members.

Decision-Making Style: From Pursuing the Optimal to Supporting the Acceptable

The decision-making style of supervisors is very different from that of frontline workers. The mission of frontline workers is to find the optimal solution for their clients. This mission is respected and supported by the profession and the community. However, supervisors, as managers, must make acceptable decisions within given time and organizational constraints (Perlmutter, 1990). Frontline workers make decisions based on information about the client's situation. Supervisors, in contrast, must choose among limited alternatives. They are required to answer "yes or no" and "multiple choice" questions within a short period of time.

Relationship Orientation: From Helping to Monitoring

The relationship orientation of supervisors is also different from that of frontline workers. Relationship building is the core of the social work profession. In interviews with frontline workers, clients are encouraged to impart private information and express genuine feelings. However, the relationship between the supervisor and the supervisee is less therapeutic and supportive (Austin, 1981). Of course, the supervisor should understand the strengths and weaknesses of the frontline workers. This information may be used, however, for professional development or even performance appraisal. As a result, supervisees feel hesitant to express their true feelings to their supervisors.

Outcome Orientation: From Service
Effectiveness to Cost Effectiveness

Frontline workers are trained to provide effective treatment of their clients in order to attain the goals of intervention. They judge their intervention from the perspective of its effectiveness. The resources required to achieve these goals are not their major concern. Their focus is on the client's acquisition of skills, the feelings expressed in the intervention process, and recognition of the importance of their own contribution. However, these effects are not easy to observe or measure. Supervisors, on the other hand, are accountable to the public and funding bodies. They must produce evidence of effective outcomes at acceptable costs. Thus, cost effectiveness (where efficiency is measured according to the ratio of output of services to input of resources), rather than service effectiveness, becomes the primary focus. This is a source of endless conflicts between supervisors and frontline workers.

Colleague Orientation: From Horizontal to Hierarchical

A collegial, peer relationship is optimal among frontline social workers. However, such horizontal relationships are replaced by hierarchical ones once a frontline worker has been promoted to the rank of supervisor. The informal, supportive, and intimate relationship is replaced by a formal, administrative, and often alienated relationship. As a result, newly appointed supervisors often find that they suffer from a loss of peer support and informal communication with colleagues. Many supervisors complain that they feel lonely and have difficulty expressing their feelings. As middle managers, they cannot talk frankly with the top management. As managers, they are distanced from the clients. As supervisors, they are constrained in their communication with subordinates.

6

Educational and Supportive Functions

This chapter will focus on the educational and supportive functions of supervision. Although these two functions are not essential for accountability to the top management of the organization and the community, they are much expected by frontline staff. The educational function can be identified in activities referred to as "teaching," "training," "staff development," "coaching," and "mentoring." Some scholars believe if the educational function were separated from the administrative function, the staff would feel free to express their difficulties and mistakes in direct practice. However, others maintain that supervisors should fulfill both functions so that they can provide appropriate administrative support and reward while offering guidance and advice.

The educational aspect of supervision encourages the staff's general development and their choice of specific areas of expertise. Supervision provides orientation to new frontline workers; it provides them with the strategies and skills necessary to deal with clients, especially involuntary clients. The developmental stage of the supervisee influences the format, structure, and purpose of supervision. More autonomy will be given to those social workers who have more practice experience. Supervisors see their educational responsibilities as a mechanism and process for developing the staff. Supervisees use supervision as an opportunity to seek the supervisor's advice concerning their interventions. If the matter relates only to procedures, the supervisee usually consults peers. If it relates to decisions, the supervisee is likely to consult a peer first and then consult the supervisor. A supervisor of a pilot service project told me that, as the service is so new, supervision provides an orientation to help the staff grasp its nature. The supervisor also uses supervision sessions to identify the training needs of the staff and discuss clinical skills in handling cases.

In 1973 and 1989, Kadushin (1974, 1992b, 1992c) conducted large-scale national surveys of social work supervision in the United States. As well as analyzing basic descriptive data, Kadushin presented the strengths and shortcomings of social work supervision identified by supervisors and supervisees (Kadushin, 1992c). He drew a large random sample of 750 supervisors and 750 supervisees from the membership of the National Association of Social Workers (NASW) of the United States. These two important sample surveys provided a representative picture of the state of the art of social work supervision in the United States. In the 1989 survey, Kadushin found that the dominant format of supervision remained the individual session. Both supervisors and supervisees considered the educational function the most important, followed by the supportive function. Evaluation of staff performance was perceived as a difficult task by both the supervisor and the supervisee. Regrettably, Kadushin (1992b) did not take the opportunity to do an in-depth analysis, for example, to use inferential statistics, for the purpose of theory building. He provided basic descriptive statistics to show current supervisory practice but did not inform supervisory practice in the future.

In an empirical study, Erera and Lazar (1994a) targeted a research population comprising nearly all the social work supervisors in Israel, including team leaders ($N = 99$), service-oriented supervisors ($N = 23$), and treatment-oriented supervisors ($N = 111$). A questionnaire on role conflict and ambiguity was administered. The study indicated that team leaders experienced more role conflict and ambiguity than treatment-oriented supervisors did, because team leaders perform multiple administrative duties and supervisory roles at the same time. Based on these findings, Erera and Lazar (1994a) examined the compatibility of the administrative and educational functions of supervision and suggested that the two should be separated. In addition, they constructed a measurement tool to operationalize Kadushin's model of supervisory functions; the resulting Supervisory Functions Inventory (SFI) was validated using the same sample as their earlier study (Erera & Lazar, 1994a). Factor analysis generated seven factors corresponding to the three supervisory functions. The factors of the administrative function are policy, planning, and budgeting; quality control; and contacts with community services. Three additional factors were associated with the educational function: professional skills and techniques; professional boundaries; and knowledge and information. Finally, support for frontline social workers was considered the seventh factor. A further univariate analysis of variance revealed that the administrative function, and not the educational or supportive function, was responsible for the differentiation among social work supervisors in various service settings (Erera & Lazar, 1994b).

> Mr. Choy elaborated on the educational function of supervision: "In terms of development of the staff, I also have the role of a teacher. I make use of the supervision session to teach the staff how to do their job."
>
> A supervisor shared his views with other supervisors in a focus group: "The purpose of supervision is to strengthen the space and autonomy (of the staff), stimulate the staff, and enhance their development."

The supervisees agreed with the supervisors that the second purpose of supervision is to teach the skills necessary to help clients effectively.

> Lily, a youth worker in a children and youth center, maintained that the goals of supervision are "to provide guidance for service delivery and to provide professional advice for staff."
>
> Sally, a frontline worker in an integrated service team for youth, said, "The supervisor will give you professional advice. It makes you do a better job."
>
> Nancy, a caseworker in a government-run family service center, observed that the supervision process allows the supervisor to get to know the work of the staff, including situations arising during case management and the difficulties encountered, and to try to help . . . to understand the career plan of the staff and their readiness to move to other units."

CHARACTERISTICS OF EDUCATIONAL SUPERVISION

Educational supervision is a teaching and learning process in which there are two partners. Both of them should be ready to give and take. In the process, a shared meaning will develop. There will be a readiness to share and a motivation to learn. As Kadushin and Harkness (2002) suggested, this requires planning and preparation. The focus of educational supervision is on the knowledge, skills, and attitudes of direct service. The supervisor acts as the resource person, giving advice and guidance. Feedback has an important place in educational supervision. However, effective feedback relies on open communication with the staff. As a result, educational supervision is sometimes perceived by social workers as "clinical supervision." Effective feedback flourishes in an atmosphere of learning and self-improvement where there is a strong sense of security. Administrative supervision focuses on what the frontline workers should be. Educational supervision focuses on what the frontline workers are. As an administrator, the supervisor is responsible for deadlines and bottom lines. However, the supervisor must also set a baseline for the development of the staff. The supervisor should make an initial assessment of the staff, identify their difficulties in direct practice, and determine their needs for professional growth. Then a tailor-made plan for educational supervision can be formulated.

GIVING FEEDBACK

Giving feedback to supervisees is an art. Kadushin and Harkness (2002) provided the following guidelines:

1. Feedback should be given as soon as possible after the performance.
2. Feedback should be as specific as possible.
3. Feedback should be objective and concrete.
4. Feedback should be descriptive rather than judgmental.
5. Feedback should highlight the effects of good performance.
6. Feedback should be focused on the behavior of the supervisee rather than on the supervisee as a person.

7. Feedback should be offered tentatively for consideration and discussion rather than authoritatively for agreement and acceptance.

8. Feedback should be tied as explicitly as possible to what you want the supervisee to learn.

9. Good feedback involves sharing ideas rather than giving advice, exploring alternatives rather than giving answers.

10. Feedback needs to be selective in terms of the amount that a person can absorb (Kadushin & Harkness, 2002, pp. 160–161)

SUPPORTIVE SUPERVISION

Supervision also provides a time and place for the supervisor to support their supervisees. It allows supervisors to show their appreciation. This supportive function is the third function of social work supervision recognized by Kadushin and Harkness (2002). Support can be emotional, as well as practical.

The supervisor's role in providing support to frontline staff is very important. Himle, Jayaratne, and Thyness (1989) conducted a sample survey of 800 social workers randomly drawn from a population of 2,664 social workers in Norway. Four aspects of the supervisory relationship were studied (psychological strains, job satisfaction and turnover, work stress, and social support) as well as four kinds of social support (emotional support, appraisals, informational support, and instrumental support). The survey indicated that the instrumental support and informational support provided by a supervisor may reduce psychological stress and, in turn, relieve burnout and job dissatisfaction of frontline social workers. Himle et al. (1989) suggested that both appraisals and emotional support are ineffective in buffering work stress, because appraisals are mainly given to improve job performance and emotional support is sometimes deflected by frontline workers as it requires too much personal disclosure. The researchers concluded that human service organizations should train supervisors to give informational and instrumental support, which enhances skill competence, especially that of new and inexperienced staff.

A supervisor described the needs of her supervisees: "The staff tells me how they do the job. In fact, they are not asking what they should do; they just need my recognition."

Charles discussed the supportive role in supervision: "Sometimes (in addition to being a supervisor) I am also a counselor. The staff is so new. The helping process is unstructured. When I am available, I talk with them about life. For example, when they quarrel with their spouse, I also share with them how I cope with it. . . . Official matters must be handled. However, if personal matters cannot be settled, official matters will suffer. If the supervisee is willing to talk to me and trusts me, with my background as a counselor, I will try to help him or her; however, we are not in the capacity of a superior and a subordinate. After our talk, their job performance will be better. Formal and informal matters cannot be totally separated. But for the kinds of personal matters they have to handle it themselves, I won't intervene. In terms of official matters, I am the supervisor, but in terms of personal matters, I am a friend."

May, a school social worker, commented that an important aspect of her supervisor's responsibilities is "to provide emotional support to the supervisees, to face the frustration . . . to understand my feelings about work. He also lets me know his feelings."

Lily, a youth worker, continued, "Another function is to relieve work pressure, to revitalize the staff, to understand the staff's feelings, and to clarify directions."

John, an experienced community worker, observed that one of the functions of supervisors is "to achieve consensus among the staff with regard to the tasks and operations of the service unit, and to enhance team-building through sharing."

Karen, a social work assistant in the rehabilitation unit of a large nongovernment organization, said, "Supervision helped to eliminate staff conflict. Everyone agrees on something and writes it down. This is a compromise process. The documents are the evidence of the consensus."

STRESS AND BURNOUT

Social work is considered a high-risk profession in terms of stress and burnout because of the high level of demands from various stakeholders. Stress is a negative feature of the environment that impinges on the individual (Shinn, Rosario, Morch, & Chestnut, 1984). Burnout is a cluster of physical and emotional maladaptive reactions to high levels of chronic work-related stress (Arches, 1991). The most common symptom of burnout is emotional exhaustion (Wallace & Brinkerhoff, 1991). The feeling of burnout, put into words, is "I give up" (Johnson, 1988). Such thoughts are a warning to workers that they no longer have the ability and willpower to carry on. Karasek and Theorell (1990) explained the existence of stress in the workplace based on the classic demand-control-support model. They put demand at one extreme of the spectrum, and support at the other. When there is a high demand at work, but a low degree of support, there will be stress and even burnout.

There are four major sources of work stress. The first is the demands of the job. Two rules apply: first, the greater the interfacing between boundaries (whether interpersonal or interorganizational), the higher the stress; second, the more uncertain the situation, the higher the stress. For example, first-line supervisors have one of the most stressful occupations because they are expected to perform a variety of demanding tasks. These include managerial tasks such as decision making, routine tasks that require the monotonous repetition of actions, boundary-spanning tasks that involve work with outsiders, and performance appraisals that require difficult decisions leading to reward or punishment. Of course, overwork and job insecurity can also increase the level of work stress. Work stress is heightened by role conflict and ambiguity. In her research on burnout among social work supervisors, Erera (1991b) discovered that the primary cause of burnout was ambiguous and incompatible organizational policies. When there is a lack of concrete and specific guidelines for decision making, a decision may not be accepted by the staff. It may even lead to interpersonal conflicts between supervisors and supervisees. Another potential source of discomfort is the physical environment. Problems with temperature, lighting, sound, and office design are tiring and annoying, and, thus, contribute to work stress. Finally, and most important, interpersonal demands create an enormous pressure on staff. Stress arises from abrasive personalities, lack of psychological space and distance, and discrepancies in rank, qualifications, and income. These conditions can lead to tense interpersonal relationships. When the working relationship is distorted by power games, colleagues will suffer.

Brown and Bourne (1996) identified the physical and behavioral signs of stress. The physical signs include fatigue without apparent expenditure of energy, loss of weight and appetite, insomnia, increased headaches, body tension such as aches and pains without apparent causes, and substance abuse. When staff exhibit such symptoms, the supervisor should pay attention and express concern. From my experience, the most effective response is to reduce staff workload immediately, in order to create the time and space for rest and recovery. However, supervisors should be careful. They should take low-key, temporary measures. Otherwise, the staff will feel that the supervisor no longer has confidence in them. In addition, they may lose face in front of their colleagues.

The behavioral signs of stress include progressive self-imposed isolation, increased indecision, excessive self-criticism, a mechanical approach to work, loss of enthusiasm, the perception of tasks as overwhelming, inertia, resistance to innovation and change, impatience and irritability, stereotyping, and breakdown in social and personal relationships (Brown & Bourne, 1996). Whenever workers exhibit such behavior, the supervisor should provide more emotional support. At this stage, one alternative is to let the worker take a break. Sometimes a vacation is all that is required. If the stress is due to a chronic situation, taking a vacation may not solve the problem, but, at least, it will temporarily reduce the burden. In addition, the supervisor's concern will be greatly appreciated by the worker. The most important rule is to let the worker make his or her choices after listening to the alternatives. Supervisors may not be aware of the whole picture. It is best to show concern and support, not to act as a counselor. Brown and Bourne (1996) suggested intervention strategies that can be adopted during the various stages of burnout.

Stage 1: Initial Enthusiasm

Sometimes, a supervisee assumes an unrealistic number of extra duties, which soon leads to an overwhelming workload. At this stage, the supervisor may review the supervisee's past work history;

identify the supervisee's strengths, weaknesses, and needs; check the potential sources of stress; and set realistic and achievable short-term and long-term goals.

Stage 2: Premature Routinization

By stage 2, the initial enthusiasm has worn off, and the job seems less exciting. The supervisor must ensure that supervisees protect themselves emotionally and successfully separate their private life from their professional life. The supervisor should reinforce small achievements to restore the supervisee's confidence and challenge the supervisee's dismissive, mechanical response to work by examining aspects of work in detail.

Stage 3: Self-Doubt

If the process continues past stage 2 without constructive guidance, the sense of stagnation will be internalized and lead the supervisee to doubt his or her own capacity. In this situation, the supervisor should follow the procedures outlined in the previous stages. This may help the supervisee regain internal strength. Of course, the supervisor should let the supervisee know what kinds of assistance are available. The supervisor should also discuss the supervisee's experience of the previous stages and clarify what the stressors are. It is important not to assume the role of therapist; otherwise, the supervisee may become dependent, and there may be undesirable transferences. The supervisor is obliged to ensure that work done by the supervisee meets the minimum standard. Possible courses of action include reallocation of cases, change of work priorities, direct mediation between parties in conflict, change of work setting or work pattern, and provision of appropriate staff development opportunities.

Stage 4: Stagnation, Collapse, or Recovery

The characteristics of stage 4 depend on the development in the previous stages. First, supervisees experience a sense of stagnation and slowly deteriorate. They become passive and depressed. If this continues without help, a crisis may arise if they encounter a stressful situation. Some may ask for help, but others may quit their job. At this stage, the supervisor should identify sources of help, including employee guidance programs. At the same time, the supervisor must assure the supervisee that he or she will be respected and treated well by the agency.

During all stages of worker burnout, the supervisor can offer four kinds of support: emotional support, appraisals, instrumental support, and informational support (Himle et al., 1989). Emotional support is expressed through warmth and friendliness. It helps the staff to release their tension and feel that someone is concerned about them. Support in the appraisal process is shown by the supervisor's approval of what the supervisee is doing. Recognition of their achievements will give supervisees a stronger sense of security in the organization. Instrumental support refers to the guidance and assistance offered by the supervisor to get the job done. Informational support is the provision of useful information to facilitate the supervisee's job and professional growth.

Newsome and Pillari (1991) gave self-administered questionnaires to 121 randomly selected social workers from the human resources department of a medium-sized city in the southeastern United States. Their survey revealed a positive correlation between job satisfaction and the overall quality of the supervisory relationship. Rauktis and Koeske (1994) surveyed 232 supervisees, chosen by random sampling, from the Southwest Division membership list of the National Association of Social Workers. They found that supportive supervision appears to have a direct and positive association with job satisfaction. The findings of these two studies emphasize the need to provide supportive supervision in order to increase staff morale and job satisfaction.

GENDER: WORKING WITH MALE
AND FEMALE SUPERVISORS

Gender is an important issue in social work supervision. Social work is a profession that employs a number of women. However, many studies show that, although the majority of social workers are female, the proportion of female social workers in managerial positions is not high (Chernesky, 1986). It is not surprising that feminists are ideologically opposed to traditional social work supervision—as Chernesky (1986) observed, it is incongruent with feminist principles and values.

Traditionally, social work supervision coordinates, directs, and monitors social work practice. Chernesky (1986) argued that, in addition to their administrative and supportive functions, supervisors also have a professionalization function—to familiarize social workers with the norms of the profession. She also identified eight problems in the traditional supervisor-supervisee relationship. First, there is no established point in time in which the supervisee is recognized as a competent and autonomous professional. Second, no differentiation is made when responding to different workers; for example, there is no differentiation between supervisees with little experience and those with a great deal of experience (Watson, 1973). Third, there are no restrictions on the subjects that may be brought up in supervision sessions. Workers may be required to expose themselves and place themselves in vulnerable positions (Levy, 1973). Fourth, although the worker is responsible for the client, the supervisor is ultimately accountable to top management (Chernesky, 1986). Fifth, the supervisor-supervisee relationship is not an egalitarian one. Sixth, the supervisor represents and interprets the actions of the supervisee to top management, and, in turn, represents and interprets the decisions of top management to the supervisee (Levy, 1973). Seventh, the integration of the administrative function and the educational function is based on the assumption that the organization's expectations are compatible with the profession's expectations. However, this is not the case. Eighth, the supervisor-supervisee relationship produces anxiety and tension.

In the traditional model of supervision, there are 11 assumptions (Chernesky, 1986). First, workers require external, organizational controls in order to do their work and to do it well. Second, if workers are not monitored on a regular basis, they will not comply with organizational mandates. Third, the commitment and internalized standards and norms of workers are not adequate to ensure their effective performance. Fourth, social workers cannot be trusted to take responsibility for the work they perform. Fifth, social workers require protection, support, and monitoring in order to perform their work. Sixth, social workers always need to learn and to be taught in order to achieve professional and personal growth and well-being and, thus, can never be independent, autonomous practitioners. Seventh, only superiors and authority figures have the knowledge, expertise, and experience to teach. Eighth, workers cannot and should not express their concerns, problems, or discontent directly to higher administration but should do this through supervisors indirectly. Ninth, authority must preside in a hierarchical arrangement; those who do must be separated from those who manage. Tenth, social workers are less capable of deciding how to implement policies than administrators. Last, a personal relationship between supervisor and supervisee is the only way to supervise and control workers (Chernesky, 1986).

Chernesky (1986) suggested an alternative feminist approach to social work supervision. First, social workers should be self-directing, self-disciplined, and self-regulating. They should be responsible for the quality of the service. A collegial relationship should replace hierarchical authority. Teaching, learning, advising, and consulting should be part of professional life. Supervision should not be the only method of monitoring job performance; records, continuous training, highly visible work, and horizontal communication can be effective substitutes. Personal growth and professional development need not depend on a teacher-pupil relationship. A process-oriented structure could be adopted. The goal of feminist social work supervision is the emergence of autonomous, self-directing, and self-regulating workers.

Some scholars (Osterberg, 1996; Powell, 1993) argue that gender differences in supervision are exaggerated because such studies focus solely on gender and assume men and women are opposites. Gender dualism has become the primary focus of study, while race, sexual orientation, age, disability status, organizational setting, and other variables are neglected or ignored. Meta-analyses of research on gender and supervision have shown gender differences in supervision to be minimal. Powell (1993) pointed out that there are not many differences between the values, needs, and supervisory styles of male and female supervisors. The differences that have been identified come primarily from laboratory studies, not field studies. Osterberg (1996) maintained that viewing gender as a primary characteristic in supervision exaggerates the significance of gender differences. In fact, more differences can be found within genders than between genders. To stress the effect of gender differences in supervisory practice and behaviors is misleading. It ignores the complexity of human behavior and identity.

Gender matching is another debatable issue. Powell (1993) raised many questions in this regard: Are there really gender differences? How can gender differences be used to provide an effective supervisory dyad? Does labeling a gender-related approach simply reinforce sexist stereotyping? In fact, the distribution of power is at the very root of gender issues (Bernard & Goodyear, 1992). The power distribution must be resolved; otherwise, the gender issue will remain an unsolved problem.

Munson (1979c) surveyed 64 supervisors and 65 supervisees identified by cluster sampling from three states in the eastern United States. He found that female supervisors are quite competent regardless of the gender of the supervisees and that there are no relationship problems between female supervisors and their male supervisees. In fact, when supervisees were asked to rate their supervisors, female supervisors received significantly higher scores than males in many areas, including nondirectiveness, helpfulness, evaluation of performance, ability to set priorities, role orientation, clinical competence, contribution to the improvement of workers' effectiveness, friendliness, ability to express appreciation, and tendency to engage in informal interaction (Munson, 1979c). In addition, females were found to be more relationship oriented and intuitive than their male counterparts, although it would be hasty to assume that men, therefore, take the task-oriented approach that is often ascribed to them. The results of Munson's survey indicate that there is no difference between male and female supervisors in areas associated with the administrative aspects of supervision.

DIVERSITY: ISSUES IN CROSS-CULTURAL SUPERVISION

Diversity has become an important issue in both direct social work service and supervision, because an increasing number of clients and social workers come from different ethnic groups, social classes, and cultures. Intercultural supervision has become very common. As Powell (1993) observed, there are several ways to address this issue. First, the supervisor must be aware of cultural differences, which may include differences in the concepts of space and time, worldviews, and even beliefs. Second, these cultural variations must be explored in relation to supervision. Unfortunately, there is a lack of literature and research on the relationship between diversity and social work supervision. Third, as culture, ethnicity, and social class may determine the patterns of help-seeking behavior on the part of clients, the supervisor and the supervisee should pay close attention to these issues.

In general, the attitude necessary to deal with the diversity issue is cultural sensitivity. The supervisor and the supervisee should respect each other's background and views. Both parties should view the difference as a natural part of life. This is especially necessary in supervisory relationships in which the supervisor and supervisee are from different social or ethnic groups. As the social work profession has turned its attention to issues of diversity in its practice, similar issues have emerged in the context of supervision and management (Shulman, 1982, 1993; *Encyclopedia of Social Work*, 1995). Concerns have been raised about the number of members of minority racial and ethnic groups who assume management roles.

7

Power Issues
Between Supervisors
and Supervisees

THE NATURE OF POWER AND AUTHORITY

In a bureaucracy, social work supervisors are, by nature, also human service managers. As managers, they must use authority and power, whether they like it or not. However, the use of authority and power is usually not welcomed by frontline social workers who value care, equality, teamwork, and staff participation. Authority and power issues have been overlooked in the literature on social work supervision. It was only in the late 1970s that Munson (1979a, 1979b, 1981) conducted his study on the use of supervisory authority.

In a well-designed study, Munson (1979a, 1979b, 1981) randomly selected 64 supervisors and 65 supervisees from social welfare agencies in three U.S. states. A self-administered questionnaire was mailed to supervisors. The data on supervisees were collected through interviews. Munson found that there was a clear and significant relationship between the use of supervisory authority and levels of interaction, supervision satisfaction, and job satisfaction. Job satisfaction and supervision satisfaction were found to be higher in situations where the supervision followed the competency model (the authority of the supervisor comes from knowledge and practice skills) than where it followed the sanction model (the authority of the supervisor is inherent in the position in the administrative hierarchy based on agency sanction). In the competence model, the supervisor must demonstrate skill competence in professional practice in order to establish professional authority and receive the recognition and acceptance of staff. In Kadushin's (1992b) study, it was found that this type of supervisor is the most highly regarded by frontline workers in the United States. Obviously, frontline social workers respect supervisors who can teach them problem-solving skills applicable to daily operations. In addition, supervisors who help frontline workers solve intervention problems are deeply appreciated.

According to the sanction model, the supervisor uses the position assigned by the organization to direct the frontline social workers to achieve the organizational objectives. However, the use of this external force sometimes creates resistance from the staff. The staff do not learn from the supervisor during the intervention process; they just follow instructions. Frontline workers tend to fulfill only the minimum requirements set by their supervisors. Eventually, frontline workers will experience little professional growth. In addition, they seldom identify with the supervisor. The supervisor becomes a manager, instead of a teacher and an enabler. When frontline workers have problems in direct practice, they do not receive informational support, technical support, or emotional support from their supervisors. The supervisor is primarily a performance appraiser, so workers are reluctant to share their troubles and genuine feelings.

THE DIFFERENCES BETWEEN POWER AND AUTHORITY

Both Munson (1981, 1993) and Kaiser (1997) recognized the importance of the use of authority and power in the supervisory relationship and emphasized the significance of the power difference between the supervisor and the supervisee. As Kaiser (1997) indicated, authority and power are two major components of the supervisory relationship. However, it is crucial to differentiate these two concepts. Kadushin and Harkness (2002) suggested that power is the ability to control others, while authority is the right to do so. As they further elaborated, "authority is a right that legitimizes the use of power. It is the sanctioned use of power, the accepted and validated possession of power.

Authority is the right to issue directives, exercise control, and require compliance. It is the right to determine the behavior of others and to make decisions that guide the action of others" (Kadushin & Harkness, 2002, p. 84). In a bureaucracy, the authority comes from the administrative structure in which there is division of labor and integration of efforts in order to achieve the organizational objectives. The assignment and use of administrative authority are necessary for daily operations. In its simplest sense, power is the ability to use authority. Kadushin and Harkness used a striking example to illustrate the difference: the hijacker of a plane has power but no authority; the prison warden held hostage by prisoners has authority but no power (Kadushin & Harkness, 2002, p.85).

THE SOURCES OF POWER AND AUTHORITY

Power can be classified according to various criteria. The most frequently used classification was developed by French and Raven (1960). They divided power into five categories: reward power, coercive power, legitimate power, referent power, and expert power. The first three kinds of power come from the organization. When supervisors use these kinds of power, they are perceived as administrators. The latter two come from the supervisor as an individual and a professional. They depend on the personal qualities and professional competence of the supervisor.

Reward power refers to the capacity of the supervisor to control the tangible rewards for the staff, including promotions, salary increases, staff development, leaves, and desirable work assignments. Reward power requires careful handling. On the one hand, the supervisor has to differentiate and individualize the rewards; otherwise, they will become routine ritual and lose their motivational force. On the other hand, the supervisor must be fair and perceived to be fair by all the staff members. If not, the frontline workers will resent the use of reward power and there will be strong staff resistance. This will reduce the productivity of the team and will be harmful to staff morale.

Coercive power is the ability of supervisors to use punishment to influence the behavior of staff members. Punishments include disciplinary actions, demotions, dismissals, and undesirable work assignments. Of course, the supervisor may also express disapproval and impose restrictions. However, as mentioned earlier, the respect for professional autonomy and societal culture make supervisors reluctant to exercise coercive power. According to Kadushin's (1992c) large-scale survey, many supervisors are hesitant to use this power: The following comments are typical:

- I do not like to confront my staff.
- I have a very hard time telling people what to do.
- I have weak limit-setting confrontation skills.
- My problem lies in confronting poor, negative performance.
- I am reluctant to give negative feedback.
- I have difficulty terminating an employee even though it might be clearly indicated.
- I find it difficult to confront supervisees on their failure to perform necessary tasks.

All supervisors want to be perceived as "nice" and to be popular among staff. Nobody wants to be hated by frontline workers.

Legitimate power comes from the official position held by the supervisor. The power is delegated by the top management to fulfill the tasks assigned by the organization. Legitimate power is impersonal. Staff members respond to the position not the person who holds it. Staff are obliged to accept this authority. However, this kind of compulsory conformity may reduce the workers' motivation, which is very important in professional practice. Productivity will be at a minimum. The use of legitimate power reminds staff that they must be obedient to authorities. It should only be used to fulfill the administrative functions of supervision.

Referent power comes from the staff's identification with the supervisor. It has two conditions: a good relationship between the supervisor and the supervisee and a clear admiration of the supervisor on the part of the supervisee. As described by Kadushin and Harkness (2002), a supervisee said, "I want to be like the supervisor and be liked by her. Consequently, I want to believe and behave as she does." And "I am like the supervisor, so I will behave and believe like her" (p. 88). Once referent power is established, the supervisor becomes one of the significant others of the supervisee. Of course, to achieve this kind of influence over supervisees, supervisors must improve personal qualities.

Expert power comes from the supervisor's knowledge and skills in social work practice. If supervisors can provide insights for future direction and make the right decisions for direct service, they will be perceived as powerful due to their expertise. Supervisees will follow their advice in professional practice. Such supervisors are influential and powerful in their field.

THE ART OF USING POWER AND AUTHORITY

Although power imbalance is evident to everyone in human service organizations, the means of handling such imbalance are not equally obvious. At one extreme, when the power difference is too great, the staff will not be motivated to try their best. At the other extreme, the power difference may be too small to allow for adequate monitoring of staff performance. In either case, there will be much tension between the supervisor and the supervisee. Kaiser (1997) described this delicate balance as a "dual relationship." On the one hand, supervisors have a "limit-setting function" to fulfill; they must ensure that the supervisee fulfills at least the minimum requirements of the job. If the supervisee fails to do so, the supervisor is expected to provide negative feedback or even a warning. This is a difficult task, one that supervisors are often reluctant to undertake. On the other hand, supervisors must construct a "shared meaning" with staff members based on a supportive relationship and effective communication.

The crux of the problem is that there is always confusion and controversy. In the delicate balance between these two functions, there are always other confounding variables that further complicate the situation. Misunderstandings may arise when the supervisor and supervisee have different ethnicities, cultures, or genders. For example, in Chinese culture, which emphasizes the acceptance of hierarchy, respect for seniority, maintenance of social status, and the pursuit of harmony, the authority of supervisors is relatively easy to establish (Tsui, 2002). However, in the United States, supervisors need to gain their authority by demonstrating their skill competence (Kadushin & Harkness, 2002).

As Kaiser (1997) noted, a key factor underlying the dynamics of supervisory authority is the attitudes toward authority. Holloway and Brager (1989) pointed out that such attitudes are based on three factors: (1) how supervisees perceive the source for power and whether they consider it legitimate; (2) how supervisees acquire desired resources (or avoid sanctions); and (3) the degree to which supervisees believe that cooperation with an authority is likely to result in access to desired resources (or avoidance of sanctions) (p. 59). These factors determine how supervisees react to supervisory styles and uses of authority. Culture is one of the significant variables contributing to the development of these attitudes.

Tsui (2001) found that the supervisor has dominant decision-making power in the supervisory process. When the supervisor and the supervisee differ, the supervisee always follows the supervisor's instruction. Only a few supervisees choose to talk with their peers and then convey their views to the supervisor. Almost all supervisors interviewed adopted a "consensus" approach to the use of their supervisory authority. They have a basic plan in mind and then they consult with the staff. In the process, supervisors let the supervisees discuss the issue but they express their own views implicitly. If the staff agree, then a decision is made collectively. If not, supervisors try to absorb the opinions of the supervisees, revise their own hidden agenda, and then sell a revised plan. In most cases, the staff do not argue with the supervisor, because they are accustomed to being respectful. In this way, the supervisor passively acquires the consent of the staff. After the consultation process, the supervisor can incorporate the views of the staff; this legitimizes the plan and also provides essential information. Of course, there are different structures and processes of using administrative authority in different organizations. In general, large human service organizations tend to have well-structured hierarchies and procedures. However, it is a common practice in both large and small organizations: for supervisors to use consultation and co-optation to manipulate the decision-making process.

When supervisors use the "consensus" approach, they divide issues into two categories. When the issues are related to agency policy or administration, the supervisor makes the decision in a straightforward way. For matters related to professional practice or service delivery, the supervisor encourages staff discussion. If the timing for service delivery is tight (e.g., in urgent cases), the supervisor makes a decision and gives specific step-by-step instructions. In less pressing situations, the supervisor allows the staff to discuss the matter among themselves. In the end, the supervisor gives clear instructions and makes sure staff members follow them. Sometimes, supervisees consult their supervisors because they want to hold their supervisors responsible for decisions. When supervisors give vague advice or tell supervisees to do it their own way, supervisees feel anxious about the results.

A supervisor said, "There are red, yellow, and green lights. First, for matters with a red light, there is no room for discussion. I make the decision, for example, annual leave or working hours. Second, for matters with a green light, the staff members make the decision. I just care about the output. For matters with a yellow light, we may discuss, for example, the direction of our service unit, the program objectives for next year, or the nature of new services."

A supervisor of a children and youth center said, "For some matters, I make the decision. For other matters, we make the decision together. I hope that we have 'consensus.' However, the staff members expect me to make the decision. After I make the decision, they are often unhappy. Supervisory authority is only an abstract power; whenever you use it, you really possess it."

A team leader of an integrated service team for youth said, "After I sell my ideas, if the staff do not buy them and the matter is not serious, I pass the decision on to the staff. For service delivery, I give staff a free hand. For administration, they have to follow my suggestion; there are no other alternatives."

A supervisor of an employee assistance program said, "Usually I consult with them, though I already have a plan. But I keep it secret. The staff do not insist on their views. If my views are totally different from their views, I tell them my ideas. To a certain extent, I would like to influence them."

From the supervisees' perspective, the supervisor adopts the "consensus" approach to make decisions. From the supervisors' perspective, the use of administrative authority in decision making is only a last resort, because it has a negative impact on staff morale. Some supervisees believe that "consensus" is only a political gesture on the part of the supervisor, so they do not speak candidly in the consultation process. Supervisees tend to give in to their supervisors most of the time. This may maintain harmony within the service unit, but it reduces staff participation and a sense of belonging.

May, a school social worker, said, "If I thought the supervisor's ideas were not good, I would tell him. If he thought my comments were reasonable, he would accept them. If he does not accept them, I agree with him and then pursue my goal in another way. Sometimes he knows. He asks why. Sometimes I explain, and sometimes I cover up."

Kevin, a social worker in an outreach team for youth, said, "My supervisor is always lobbying. She discusses matters with us privately. The decisions are made in the working group. I feel that the supervisor spends a lot of time pursuing this kind of decision making. It is very difficult."

Cindy, a medical social worker, said, "Usually, the supervisor makes the decision. He chooses the best alternative, except when the matter is in the process of implementation. Then, if we have different views, we discuss them. There may be some modification. But usually the supervisor's view dominates."

SUPERVISORS' AND SUPERVISEES' POWER GAMES

The power game, by nature, is an uncooperative game. It is a delicate and subtle form of confrontation and competition. The basis of the power game is a lack of trust and consensus. In a power game, there must be two parties. However, the participants are opponents, not partners. Both parties would like to gain advantages. They want maximum benefits with minimum cost. In the process, there are complicated strategies and tactics. No matter who wins the game, the outcome is that everyone is the loser in terms of effectiveness of supervision. The purposes and functions of professional supervision can never be achieved in these circumstances.

SUPERVISORS' GAMES

Games of Abdication

When supervisors feel that they do not have adequate administrative support or professional competence to exercise their supervisory authority, they often play the game of abdication (Hawthorne, 1975).

This game involves passing the responsibilities for administrative decisions and professional input on to somebody else, sometimes top management and sometimes even frontline staff. In these cases, the supervisor deliberately confuses professional and personal identities. According to Hawthorne (1975) and Kadushin (1979), there are five games of abdication played by supervisors: "They won't let me," "Poor me," "I'm really one of you," "One good question deserves another," and "I wonder why you really said that." An elaboration of each follows.

"They won't let me"

In this game, the supervisor pretends that he or she is willing to let the supervisee take action. However, the supervisee's act will not be approved by top management. The supervisor is passing the buck and, at the same time, surrendering his or her power and losing the respect of their subordinates. Frontline social workers are critical of this kind of supervisor, who is perceived as a mouthpiece of top management. Such supervisors will not protect their subordinates or protest against unreasonable requests from top management.

"Poor me"

In this case, supervisors complain about their position. They are so busy: there are so many demands from different parties. Due to heavy administrative burdens, there is no time to conduct meaningful supervisory sessions or meetings with frontline social workers. It appears that these supervisors are seeking the sympathy of their staff. This reversal of roles encourages supervisees to see their supervisor as a client in need of help. The supervisee may feel obligated to support and protect the supervisor. Such supervisors provide no administrative leadership, professional advice, or even emotional support.

"I'm really one of you," or "I'm really a nice guy"

These are two similar situations. In "I'm really one of you," supervisors align themselves with their supervisees by proclaiming that they are against the policy and regulations of the organization. They try to convince their staff that they are just another member of the peer group. In "I'm really a nice guy," the supervisor's main goal is pleasing the frontline staff on the basis of personal, rather than professional, merits. Supervisors try to convince their staff that they are nice, attractive, friendly, and sociable. Both of these games allow supervisors to avoid their administrative and professional responsibilities.

"One good question deserves another"

In this situation, the supervisor always asks what the supervisee thinks. This tactic passes the burden of decision making on to the supervisee. No useful advice is provided. The supervisor may ask the supervisees to collect more information or conduct further research. Supervisees then feel that they have raised a significant issue. The supervisor must think highly of them to grant them so much autonomy. In fact, such supervisors are avoiding their professional and administrative responsibilities and deferring their supervisory tasks indefinitely.

The game of abdication may encourage independent thinking and professional autonomy, but crucial aspects of the supervisory relationship—administrative accountability, professional advice, emotional support—will suffer. When parties maintain the appearance of respect, the relationship may continue in a superficial manner. However, this kind of supervisory relationship is not an effective way of monitoring quality of service, a valuable means of professional growth, or a meaningful interpersonal relationship.

"I wonder why you really said that"

Kadushin (1979) identified this game in which supervisors use a very defensive attitude. They recast the supervisees' honest disagreement as psychological resistance. This distortion allows the supervisor to avoid using research evidence, practice examples, or professional literature in debates with supervisees. This defensive tactic transfers the responsibility of soliciting evidence from the supervisor to the supervisee. Then the supervisor is released from the burden of supporting his or her view with solid arguments.

Games of Power

Some games are based on assertions of power rather than on abdication of responsibility. Hawthorne (1975) identified the following:

"Remember who's the boss," "I'll tell on you," "Father/mother knows best," and "I'm only trying to help you."

"Remember who's the boss"

In this game, the supervisor wields absolute administrative power. There is no room for negotiation or disagreement. No staff participation in decision-making is allowed. The supervisee is merely an employee who must submit to the authority of the superior. Obedience is the most valued trait. The supervisor may tell the supervisee, "Everyone in my office follows my instructions." It seems as if the unit belongs to the supervisor. It is private property, not a public organization. Of course, if supervisors want to win this game, they must be very senior in the organization. They rely on a bureaucracy that has a rigid structure and a harsh, even abusive, organizational culture.

"I'll tell on you"

Hawthorne (1975) identified this game in which the supervisor repeatedly threatens to report concerns to a higher authority. The supervisor's intention to instill fear by invoking power to punish that rests with a higher level of authority. In order to play this power game successfully, the supervisor must periodically repeat and renew the threats. Of course, such threats must be supported by a power hierarchy that only recognizes power that comes from organizational sanctions and that discourages staff participation. Some supervisors like to play this game because it appears to extend their powers beyond their true boundaries.

"Father/mother knows best"

In this game, the supervisor tries to personalize the supervisory relationship. The supervisor plays the role of father or mother. They appear to love and protect their supervisees. However, such a relationship distorts the nature of professional supervision, which builds competence and encourages professional growth. This form of parental control limits the development of the supervisee. In fact, it "infantizes" the supervisee. Experience, status, and seniority are emphasized. Although the supervisor may claim that such a relationship is for the supervisee's own good, the supervisee does not benefit.

"I'm only trying to help you," or "I know
you really can't do it without me"

Hawthorne (1975, p. 201) observed that this game is a pseudo-benevolent concern based on the assumption of the supervisee's inferior or incompetent performance. In this game, the ability of the supervisee is belittled. If the intervention is successful, the credit will be given to the supervisor. If there are any problems, they are due to the incompetence of the supervisee. The supervisor, assuming that the supervisee is inadequate and helpless, transforms the supervisory relationship into a worker-client relationship.

SUPERVISEES' GAMES

Kadushin (1979) identified four strategies that supervisees use to manipulate their supervisor: manipulating demand levels, redefining the relationship, reducing the power disparity, and controlling the situation.

Manipulating Demand Levels

"Two against the agency," or "seducing for subversion"

Kadushin (1979) observed that this game is always played by intelligent and gifted supervisees who do not like the routine administrative procedures such as submitting periodical service statistics and preparing program proposals. The supervisees argue that there is a significant conflict between bureaucratic requirements and professional values. They also claim that the administrative procedures should be ignored for the benefit of clients. Sometimes, their arguments sound reasonable and convincing. Professional autonomy is used as an excuse for not carrying out necessary procedures. However, if the supervisor is convinced, he or she may subvert organizational policy and procedures. The supervisor is no longer accountable to top management, the community, and the funding sources.

"Be nice to me because I am nice to you"

Another game played by supervisees is "Be nice to me because I am nice to you" (Kadushin, 1979). The major tactic used here is to seduce the supervisor by flattery. For example, the supervisee may tell the supervisor

- "You are always helpful."
- "You are the supervisor I am looking for."
- "You are the best supervisor I have ever met."
- "You are my teacher and friend."
- "I would not achieve this without your guidance."

Such compliments put the supervisor on a pedestal. It is difficult to reject such flattery, but if supervisors acknowledge it, they fall into the trap. They can never assert their administrative authority again.

Redefining the Relationship

"Protect the sick and the infirm," or "Treat me. Don't beat me"

In this game, supervisees emphasize their own inferiority in order to appeal to the supervisor's sympathy. The supervisor then transforms the supervisory relationship from that of teacher and student in an administrative hierarchy to that of worker and client in a therapeutic setting (Kadushin, 1979, p. 186). This game appeals to the inner motivation of the supervisor to help. Many supervisors miss the opportunity to provide therapy. This game allows supervisors to feel that they are really helping others. Such feelings of intimacy and appreciation are difficult to resist.

"Evaluation is not for friends"

In this game, the supervisory relationship is redefined by the supervisee as a social relationship rather than a professional relationship (Kadushin, 1979). The supervisee repeatedly crosses personal boundaries. The relationship between the supervisor and the supervisee begins to resemble a friendship. As a result, supervisors find it difficult to correct supervisees or to evaluate their work in a fair and objective way. Of course, there can be friendship among colleagues, but if supervisors cannot set appropriate limits, they will be manipulated by supervisees. The consequences are unfair to other colleagues, to the organization, to the funding sources, and, eventually, to the clients.

"Maximum participation"

In this game, the supervisory relationship is transformed by the supervisee into a peer relationship (Kadushin, 1979). The supervisee will cite democratic principles as an excuse for relaxing administrative arrangements: everything should be equal between the supervisor and the supervisee. The pretense is established that there is no difference between the duties of the supervisor and those of the supervisee; they are just colleagues. However, there are differences in expectations, accountabilities, and authorities assigned by the top management, funding sources, and clients. If there were not, there would be no need to create the position of supervisor.

Reducing the Power Disparity

"If you knew Dostoyevsky, like I know Dostoyevsky"

The supervisee's strategy here is to test the supervisor's knowledge outside the field of his or her expertise. The supervisee's questions may be related to history, literature, or therapy. If supervisors do not want to confess their ignorance, they will have to play the game (Kadushin, 1979). The supervisee will instruct the supervisor, reversing their customary roles. The supervisee may further test the supervisor by asking, "You remember, don't you?" This game is based on the assumption that the supervisor must be more knowledgeable than the supervisee in all areas.

"So what do you know about it?"

In this game, supervisees claim to know more than the supervisor. For example, a supervisee may maintain that he or she knows more about a client than the supervisor. A female frontline worker may insist that she knows more about women than a male supervisor. A supervisee who has two children may claim that she knows more about children than a supervisor without children. Older supervisees may refer to their rich life experiences. A young frontline worker may argue that the supervisor is ignorant of popular culture. Again, the roles of the supervisor and the supervisee are reversed.

"Putting the supervisor down," or "Telling it like it is"

In this situation, supervisees use verbal violence. They swear in front of the supervisor, using the excuse that they are simply repeating what the client said. This behavior may make the supervisor uncomfortable and may shift the balance of power between the supervisor and the supervisee. These abusive supervisees argue that the remedial orientation of the social work profession is useless. They advocate a complete revolution of the profession. Because their remarks often have a partial validity, the supervisor may be made to feel like a hypocrite.

Controlling the Situation

"I have a little list"

A supervisee playing this game spends a great deal of time discussing something that is not relevant to the supervision session but may be of interest to the supervisor. The supervisee pretends to listen, but he or she may not really be interested (Kadushin, 1979). The point is to hijack the supervision session. By raising irrelevant questions, the supervisee controls the direction and content of the session.

"Heading them off at the pass"

Supervisees open the session by confessing all the mistakes they committed in the intervention process. The supervisor has no choice but to react sympathetically. The supervisor feels obliged to identify the supervisees' strengths in order to cheer them up. This game diverts any rational discussion of the intervention process. There will be no critical review of the intervention and no productive search for means of improvement.

"Little old me"

The assumption of this game is that the supervisee is completely ignorant and innocent, and, therefore, the supervisor is obliged to proceed step by step. This game increases the supervisee's dependence on the supervisor. The supervisor has difficulty exercising supervisory authority.

"I did what you told me"

The supervisee passes the responsibility for professional intervention to the supervisor. The supervisee only follows the supervisor's instruction. If the intervention fails, the supervisee can blame the supervisor.

"It's all so confusing"

The supervisee's tactic is to appeal to various authorities. This strategy is intended to reduce the authority of the supervisor. Other authorities may include former supervisors, top management, experts in the field, and social work professors.

"What you don't know won't hurt me"

Supervisees use a distancing technique to reduce the authority of the supervisor; they claim that the supervisor cannot appreciate the real conditions of frontline service. That means the supervisor has no right to give instructions.

HOW TO DEAL WITH POWER GAMES

Power games are played when there is lack of cooperation and trust between the supervisor and the supervisee. The games themselves are uncooperative. As Kadushin and Harkness (2002) pointed out, the simple, effective, and direct methods of dealing with power games is to refuse to play. In a power game, there must be two parties. If one of the parties refuses to play, the game cannot be sustained. When a supervisor plays a game of abdication, supervisees may express their need for professional guidance explicitly and persistently in a genuine and gentle way. A counter-game response may appeal to the supervisor's sense of professional expertise. When supervisors assert their authority, of course, the supervisee adopts a forceful attitude. However, my experience suggests that there will always be conflicts with unhappy endings. Supervisors should develop a balanced authority. They are responsible for providing professional guidance. The supervisee should focus the discussion on professional practice, not personal behavior.

8

The Stages, Strategies, and Skills of Supervision

THE STAGES OF THE SUPERVISORY PROCESS

The stage of the supervision is one of the components that determine the supervisor-supervisee relationship and supervisory strategies and skills. The process of supervision in social work can be divided into stages—each with a different emphasis. This makes it easier for supervisors to focus their efforts on improving professional competence, enhancing staff morale, and providing emotional support to their supervisees.

There are four significant empirical studies. First, Granvold (1977) studied the supervisory leadership of 108 supervisors randomly drawn from the personnel of the Texas Department of Public Welfare. He divided the sample into three groups according to their service areas: financial services, social services, and support services. The study indicated that, although social service supervisors had the highest educational level and the largest number of master's degrees of the three groups, all the groups possessed similar supervisory styles (Granvold, 1977). This suggests that education does not have a significant impact on supervisory style. Formal professional training is the least important factor in preparing supervisors for their job responsibilities. From the same group of supervisors, Granvold (1978a, 1978b) found that there is a positive relationship between consideration (the extent to which a supervisor is likely to feel mutual trust, respect, and warmth in the supervisory relationship) and supervisory procedures supporting worker autonomy, responsibility, self-initiative, participation in agency operations, and independent decision making. He also found a positive relationship between organizational structure and supervisory procedures, including the use of regular, formal conferences, written communication with supervisees, reviews of agency effectiveness through follow-up records, and implementation of time studies.

In the second study, Dendinger and Kohn (1989) revised the Supervisory Skills Inventory (SSI) that was originally developed for assessing the generic skills of supervisors in business and industry. The SSI was administered to 50 social work supervisors and 238 supervisees. This validated instrument consisted of 12 domains: setting goals, planning and organizing, directing and delegating, solving problems, enforcing work rules, relating to and supporting staff, maintaining equipment, building teams, assuring safety, evaluating performance, training and coaching, and handling stress. The SSI generates evaluations of effectiveness, interest in improvement, handling negative feedback, relating to others, and commitment to the organization. The SSI was validated for assessing the strengths and identifying the areas of improvement for social work supervisors.

The third study, conducted by York and Hastings (1985), surveyed the total staff of three county social service departments in North Carolina ($N = 172$). They found that the effectiveness of supportive supervision did not increase according to the level of worker maturity. Finally, York and Denton (1990) surveyed 93 social workers in an unspecified state by mailed questionnaires. Respondents were asked to rate the overall performance of their supervisors and to describe the extent to which these supervisors exhibited 20 leadership qualities. The results suggest that the key predictor of the performance of social workers is the communication skills of the supervisor.

THE DEVELOPMENTAL STAGES OF THE SUPERVISOR

As the literature on the developmental stages of social work supervisors is scant, some of the ideas in this section are based on the literature on the development of clinical supervisors. There are four well-developed models of supervisor development in psychotherapy.

First, Alonso (1983) delineated three stages in a supervisor's career: novice, mid-career, and later career. At each stage, the supervisor struggles with three issues: the interpsychic relationship with self and identity, the interpersonal relationship between the supervisor and the supervisee, and the socio-political relationship between the supervisor and the top management. Alonso (1983) strongly believed that supervisors can and should grow throughout their professional life. Of course, a clear goal and mission are necessary. At each stage, there will be conflicts, so cooperation between the supervisor and the supervisee is necessary.

The second model, proposed by Hess (1986, 1987), also contains three stages: the beginning, the exploration, and the confirmation of the supervisor's identity. In the beginning stage, supervisors try to adjust to the transition from a frontline practitioner to a supervisor. Chapter 5 of this book contains a detailed discussion on the change of roles from frontline practitioner to supervisor. During the exploration period, supervisors go through a transition period and take supervision seriously as a meaningful activity. In the confirmation stage, supervisors consolidate their identity and focus on the needs of the supervisee. During the process, the focus shifts gradually from the self to the process and, finally, to others. Supervisors who have reached the confirmation stage are mature and considerate; they are both a teacher and a friend of the supervisee.

The third model is Stoltenberg and Delworth's (1987) four-level model of supervisor development consisting of level 1, level 2, level 3, and level 3 integrated. At level 1, supervisors tend to be highly motivated but highly dependent on their superiors. Their attention is focused more on their own needs than on the needs of the supervisee and the client. They still lack confidence and skills. At level 2, there is a great deal of conflict and ambivalence as the supervisor struggles between autonomy and dependence. At level 3, the supervisor begins to find a balance between self and others. Those who achieve level 3 integrated are "master supervisors" or "supervisors of supervisors." Supervision at this level smoothly integrates practice skills and service quality. However, the development from level 3 to level 3 integrated is very slow; it usually takes a long period of time.

According to Watkins's (1990, 1993) supervision complexity model, there are four stages in the process of adopting the supervisory role: role shock, role recovery and transition, role consolidation, and role mastery. At the role shock stage, novice supervisors are faced with their weaknesses and inadequacies. They are anxious and lack confidence. Supervisors feel better in the role recovery and transition stage, but they still feel inadequate. At the third stage, role consolidation, the supervisors' confidence has increased; they know how to use supervision skills and balance their needs. In the final stage, role mastery, there is greater consolidation of skills, quality of service, and responsibilities.

Because the four models of supervisor development mentioned previously are very similar, Heid (1997) proposed an integrated model of supervisor lifespan development. She sets the following baselines:

1. a professional identity;

2. a consistent level of confidence and competence;

3. professional autonomy;

4. healthy narcissistic needs;

5. a balanced focus on self and other;

6. an acknowledgement of the power differential inherent in the supervisory relationship;

7. an understanding of the supervisor's impact on the supervisee; and

8. a realistic identification of competencies and strengths (Heid, 1997, p. 147).

Based on the preceding baselines, Heid (1997) also formulated 10 supervisor development strands as follows:

1. sense of identity as a supervisor;

2. feeling of confidence as a supervisor;

3. degree of felt autonomy and/or dependence on others;

4. use of power and authority with supervisees, including the methods and process of supervisee evaluations;

5. degree of structure, flexibility, and variety of intervention;

6. focus on the needs of the supervisees and/or self;

7. degree of personal investment in supervisee and client success;

8. emphasis on and use of the supervisory relationship and the process of supervision;

9. degree of awareness and appraisal of the impact of self on the supervisory relationship and process; and

10. degree of realistic appraisal of competencies and limitations, coupled with an awareness and containment of personal issues, biases, and counter-transference reactions (Heid, 1997, p. 147).

Stevens, Goodyear, and Robertson (1997) examined the influence of a supervisor's experience (time served) and training (formal instruction) on supervisory stance, emphasis, and efficacy. Current thinking (Hess, 1987; Watkins, 1993) suggests that, as supervisors develop, they show more support to supervisees, demonstrate higher levels of self-efficacy, and are less critical and dogmatic. Experience and training are positively associated with changes in supervisors' self-efficacy. The results of the study by Stevens et al. (1997) suggest that more supportive, less critical, and less dogmatic approaches to supervision are a result of specific training in supervision. Thus, it would appear that experience alone is not sufficient to enhance a supervisor's development.

To summarize, supervisors must go through several stages of development, whether they like it or not. As novice supervisors, they must face the transition from the role of direct practitioner to that of supervisor. When supervisors take up managerial duties, they become service managers. When supervisors adjust to managerial work and achieve a balance between managerial and professional responsibilities, they become mature supervisors. By the final stage, supervisors are free to devote their attention to the personal needs and emotions of their supervisees.

THE DEVELOPMENTAL STAGES OF THE SUPERVISEE

Supervisees also go through various stages of professional development. In the first stage, supervisees undergo orientation and job induction. They experience a great deal of anxiety while establishing work patterns and grasping the basic level of skills in professional practice. At this stage, the supervisor should first offer emotional support, in order to help the supervisee feel secure and comfortable.

Otherwise, the supervisee will not be open to opportunities for growth. For example, the supervisor should encourage the supervisee to ask questions no matter how silly or offensive the questions may be. The supervisee should then provide the information necessary for day-to-day service. The second stage is reached when the supervisee completes the orientation and job induction stage and becomes an autonomous social worker. This signifies the development from dependence to independence. At this stage, the supervisee will have a high level of autonomy in professional practice. In the third stage, the supervisor must help the supervisee become a member of the service team; this reflects the development from independence to interdependence. In the fourth stage, the supervisee is familiar with the service technology of direct practice and, with the supervisor's help, develops an area of specialization. Through this process of professional development, job satisfaction and staff morale increase. In the final stage, the supervisor should prepare the supervisee for future development as a mentor or a supervisor. The supervisor should consider not only professional or administrative factors but also the personal aspirations of the supervisee.

THE DEVELOPMENTAL STAGES
OF THE SUPERVISORY PROCESS

In this section, Shulman's (1993) interactional model of social work supervision is adopted as the framework for discussion. In his book, *Interactional Supervision,* Shulman (1993) outlined four stages of supervision: the preliminary stage, the beginning stage, the work stage, and the termination stage.

The Preliminary Stage

The preliminary stage lays the foundation for the relationship between the supervisor and the supervisee. Shulman (1993) maintained that the most important skill for a supervisor is "tuning-in," developing a degree of preliminary empathy by putting oneself in the situation of the supervisee. In order to "tune in," the supervisor must become familiar with the background of the supervisee, including his or her values, culture, orientation, expertise, habits, and even hobbies. The supervisor should start "where the supervisee is," not "where the supervisee should be"; the supervisor should not take certain skills for granted or have unreasonable expectations. To achieve this goal, the supervisor should address issues directly and also communicate with the supervisee freely.

The Beginning Stage

In the beginning stage, the most important issue is the establishment of agreement and mutual trust between the supervisor and the supervisee. This can be achieved through a written supervisory contract or a verbal agreement. Shulman (1993) suggested that supervisors share their sense of purpose, describe their roles, collect feedback from supervisees on their perceptions, and discuss mutual obligations and expectations. The context of a supervisory contract was discussed in Chapter 4. The context may be even more important than the content of the supervisory contract. If there is no trust between the supervisor and the supervisee, a supervisory contract is a document without meaning.

The Work Stage

The work stage is the core phase of the supervisory process. The skills acquired in the work stage include sessional tuning-in skills, sessional contracting skills, elaborating skills, empathic skills, sharing skills, assertive skills (necessary to make demands and to point out obstacles), skills in sharing data, and sessional ending skills (Shulman, 1993, pp. 79–133).

Sessional tuning-in skills

The tuning-in skills in the preliminary stage can also be applied to the work stage. The essence of tuning in, according to Shulman (1993), is to face problems, not to avoid them. The supervisor must concentrate on the specific problems that the supervisee has encountered. It may be an organizational policy that is inconvenient for the staff or work-related stress. The supervisor should not place these problems at the bottom of the agenda of the supervision session. Instead, they should be the subject of focused discussion, a discussion that will enable the supervisee to express his or her underlying feelings and deal with the anger. This process will enable the supervisor and supervisee to develop mutual trust and effective communication. Of course, both the supervisor and the supervisee must possess a sincere attitude and positive motivation.

Sessional contracting skills

Although there may be a supervisory contract governing the objectives, roles, responsibilities, format, and structure of supervision, the content of each supervision session is determined by agreements made from time to time between the supervisor and the supervisee. The supervisor should take the tabled agenda as a tentative one. A more pressing concern may be apparent in the first 15 minutes of discussion. Urgent items may be added to the agenda, or they may be raised at the end of the supervision session. During the discussion, supervisors should refrain from providing solutions to the problems raised by supervisees until they know exactly what the supervisees are thinking and feeling. Sincerity, not skill, is the most important element in the process. Supervisors must maintain their authority without insisting on it. In most cases, listening is even more important than giving advice or information, especially when a supervisor is dealing with experienced frontline social workers. Supervisors must be good listeners. Otherwise, their advice will be met with great psychological resistance.

Elaborating skills

Shulman (1993) noted that there are five types of skills that a supervisor should develop in order to encourage elaboration of the issues raised by the supervisee. The first is to move from general areas to specific topics. Like a counselor in a clinical setting, the supervisor listens and then asks what, how, when, who, and where. The second skill is containment: the supervisor refrains from action and remains quiet while listening and trying to understand fully the issues raised by the supervisee. The third skill is focused listening. The supervisor must concentrate on the major concern of the supervisee and try to share the supervisee's feelings. It is necessary to understand fully the key issue and the supervisee's reaction to it. The fourth skill is questioning, which is used to acquire more specific information about the issues faced by the supervisee. A question may also serve as a good response to unexpected questions raised by the supervisee. The appropriate use of questions can help the supervisor to collect information, provide support, and give instructions. The fifth skill is the ability to remain silent when silence is appropriate. It implies that the listener is not satisfied with the answer or needs more information. It is also a strategy that encourages the supervisee to continue the dialogue.

Empathetic skills

Empathy is one of the most important and necessary qualities of social workers. The supervisor should identify with the supervisee and remove any obstacles to empathic response. Then, the supervisor must reach, acknowledge, and articulate the worker's feelings (Shulman, 1993). There is no need for supervisors to pretend that they are strong people. There is no need for them to keep their distance from staff. Supervisors should take the initiative in showing concern. When supervisees share their feelings, the supervisor must respond naturally. In this situation, understanding the difference between "becoming" and "being" is very crucial. "Becoming" sees everything as a natural process, while "being" perceives everything as a task to complete. In addition, the supervisor should make it clear that professional independence is not a must and professional interdependence is not a shame. Once again, remember to start "where the staff is," not "where the staff should be." This acknowledgment of feelings reassures supervisees that their responses are natural. Finally, it may be helpful if the supervisor summarizes the situation that the supervisee faces. This articulation will make the supervisee realize that the supervisor understands what he or she feels. Based on my experience, it is clear that supervisees greatly appreciate this acceptance. They will see you as a human supervisor.

Skills in sharing feelings

Supervision is both a professional and a personal practice. In order to share feelings, the supervisor must be "a genuine person." The supervisor should express his or her hopes and fears with smiles and tears. Do not force your supervisee to confide in you; take the initiative to share your feelings. This behavior will encourage the supervisee to be open and sincere. Supervisors may show vulnerability just as ordinary people do. When appropriate, supervisors can also show their anger over something unfair or unreasonable. This allows the supervisee to see that the supervisor is a genuine and sincere person. An effective supervisor must adopt two conflicting roles. The first is to provide warm emotional support to the staff, and the second is to ensure that the staff attain the expected level of job performance. Supervisors do not need to be perfect or preferred; they are people with strengths and weaknesses, who must reconcile their personal and professional identities.

Assertive skills: Demanding work

As the ultimate objective of supervision in social work is to provide effective and efficient service to clients, the supervisor must monitor the progress of the supervisee. Specific questions should be asked to ensure that the work is done and to monitor the manner in which it is done. The supervisor must see to it that the staff meet the job requirements. Limit-setting skills are important. They allow the supervisee to recognize expectations and demands. A series of questions will help clarify the difficulties, motivations, and feelings of the supervisee.

Skills in pointing out obstacles

There are a number of sensitive issues that may hinder the progress of the supervision session. The most common problem is the power difference between the supervisor and the supervisee in the human service organization. However, the supervisor should be aware that there are many issues that belong to the private life of the supervisee. Another skill is to focus on job performance, not personality. Otherwise, the human rights of the supervisee may be violated. If the supervisor needs to encourage the supervisee to work harder, he or she should specify the expected outcome of the work and clarify the resources available to the staff.

Skills in sharing data

Providing useful information that enables the supervisee to do the job effectively is part of the supervisor's duty. To share data in such a way that the supervisee feels encouraged to ask questions is important. If this does not happen, there will be little communication or genuine discussion. As mentioned before, informational support is as important as emotional support. Both research findings and practice experience show that helping a supervisee solve intervention problems is the most important form of support.

Sessional ending skills

Ending a supervision session is an art, as Shulman (1993) observed. The supervisor should summarize what has been discussed. The discussion may also include some working guidelines. The supervisor needs to identify the next steps required to fulfill the agreed-upon goals. If the problem raised by the supervisee requires specific practical skills, rehearsal may be useful. Finally, the supervisor must be alert for "doorknob" communications where the supervisee raises important issues at the very end of the supervision session. These communications suggest that a rearrangement of the format, structure, and agenda of the supervision session is necessary.

The Termination Stage

In the termination stage, the supervisor summarizes the various stages of the entire supervisory process and provides an account of what supervisees have learned and how they have grown. In addition, the supervisor should conduct a review of the supervisee's strengths and weaknesses. This helps the supervisee to rise to challenges in the future.

Final interviews, or exit interviews, should be arranged for those supervisees who are leaving due to promotion, further study, resignation, or retirement. Supervisors should summarize what both parties have accomplished and express their feelings about the ending of the supervisory relationship. Even the most confident supervisee has some anxiety about the separation and uncertainty about the future. The supervisor should also express appreciation for the effort that the supervisee has put into the supervisory process. This discussion serves as a basis for another beginning for both the supervisor and the supervisee.

THE RELATIONSHIP BETWEEN SUPERVISOR AND SUPERVISEE: A TRANSACTIONAL ANALYSIS

In the famous book *I'm OK, You're OK,* Harris (1967) used the notion of transactional analysis to categorize the ego states of human beings as parent, adult, and child. As Bennett (1976) observed, the parent represents standards and norms. In this ego state, the mind focuses on "should be" and "how to." In the adult ego state, the mind processes data, estimates possibilities, and makes decisions based on the reality of the environment. When people are in the child ego state, they relate to the world emotionally. They want to be instantly gratified, feel comfortable, and receive instead of give. They wish to be liked and to be taken care of by others. There are three kinds of supervisor-supervisee relationships that can be identified in terms of transactional analysis. When the supervisor-supervisee relationship follows the parent-child pattern, the supervisor dominates all decision making and gives instructions to the supervisee. In this situation, the supervisee will probably fail to achieve professional autonomy and practice competence. Atherton (1986) suggested that the supervisor-supervisee relationship should follow an adult-adult pattern with mutual trust and respect. Both the supervisor and the supervisee have "face" and dignity. He also suggested that listening is very important, because it is a way to show empathy, warmth, and support. It is the most effective indicator of the state of the supervisory relationship.

Transference can often occur within the supervisor-supervisee interaction. The supervisor should watch out for irrelevant thoughts and feelings. Atherton (1986) suggested that supervisors should ask one simple question, "What would the supervisee say about the supervisor-supervisee relationship here and now?" This relationship is commonly compared to "parent and child," "teacher and student," and "caseworker and client." The supervisor has to be alert to the possibility of transference. It may help the supervisor and the supervisee to build a close relationship; however, it may also hinder professional growth and administrative accountability.

GROUP SUPERVISION

Group supervision refers to a wide range of activities, including planning meetings, team meetings, and case conferences. Group supervision uses a group setting and a group process to implement the functions of supervision, administrative, educational, and supportive (Brown & Bourne, 1996; Kadushin & Harkness, 2002). It is not only content specific and content sensitive (Brown & Bourne, 1996, p. 145), but also context specific and context sensitive. For example, Chinese social workers tend to use group supervision to achieve a consensus among staff members (Tsui, 2001).

Next to individual supervision sessions, group supervision is the second most common type of supervision (Kadushin, 1992b; Kadushin & Harkness, 2002; Ko, 1987). However, before the supervisor decides to use group supervision, he or she must ask the following questions proposed by Munson (2002):

1. Will it be defined as supervision or peer consultation?

2. What methods will be used to get practitioners to risk exposure in group supervision, and how will anxiety about such risk be handled?

3. How will competitiveness be handled?

4. How will overly verbal and reticent members be handled?

5. How do you deal with the different backgrounds and skill levels of practitioners in the group?

6. How will case monitoring be handled?

7. What are the advantages of group supervision in comparison to individual supervision?

8. How will transference and counter-transference material be handled?

9. What techniques will be used to initiate the supervision successfully?

10. Who will be supervised in the group or groups?

11. How large will the group be?

12. What day and time will the group meet?

13. What limits will be set on the group, and how will they be presented?

14. How will resisters be handled?

15. What impact will the group have on other elements of the agency or organization?

16. Who will be responsible for setting the agenda?

17. How many supervisors will be in the group?

18. How many groups will be used?

19. What are the main purposes for establishing a group?

20. How will the goals of group supervision differ from the goals of individual supervision?

21. In what different ways will the supervisor interact in group supervision and in individual supervision?

22. How will the supervisor structure the group?

23. How will feedback be channeled?

24. How will group commitment and identity be fostered?

25. What kind and amount of record-keeping will be done?

26. How will therapy be avoided, if it is to be avoided?

27. How will the group be used to improve working relationships?

28. Should the supervisor present cases?

29. How will poor presentation be handled?

30. Will the group be time-limited or open-ended? (Munson, 2002, p. 203)

According to Brown and Bourne (1996), before the supervisor decides to use group supervision, he or she must make sure that the answers to the previous questions are resolved. To implement group supervision, the supervisor should be clear about the boundaries of group supervision, including the duration, frequency, regularity, membership, attendance requirements, rules of confidentiality, and differentiation. In a group supervision session, the supervisor is a leader of the group. He or she must be sure about the agenda and the content of discussion. An appropriate structure and a mechanism for encouraging staff participation are needed; in the group process, members should be assigned different roles. For example, an experienced frontline social worker may be invited to share his or her experiences with other members.

In a group supervision session, the supervisor has to design a structure to set the focus and use the time wisely, clarify the content for discussion, and facilitate staff participation and interaction. In terms of process facilitation, it is important to be clear who is supervising what:

1. the supervision of individuals within a group/team setting by the supervisor

2. the supervision of individuals by the group/team

3. the supervision of the group/team as a whole by the supervisor and

4. the supervision of the group/team by themselves (Brown & Bourne, 1996, p. 150).

Again, the choice may be one of relative emphasis, and that emphasis may change during the development of the group. Compared to individual supervision, group supervision as a forum allows for a much wider use of methods, for example, role-playing, small group discussion, and brainstorming.

It would seem that group supervision is an effective format for supervising social workers. However, it has advantages as well as disadvantages. Brown and Bourne (1996) summarize them as follows:

Advantages

1. The opportunity to make use of a wider variety of learning experiences

2. The opportunity for supervisees to share their experiences

3. Emotional support

4. Safety in numbers

5. Opportunity to compare and contrast own experiences and practices with others

6. Can help foster team or group cohesion and identity

7. Opportunity for supervisor to see supervisees in a different kind of relationship

8. Opportunity for supervisor to become aware of potential problems that derive from and relate to the unit/project/team

9. Allows for responsibilities, functions and roles of the supervisory process to be separated and delegated among a number of people

10. Peer influence may make modification of behavior more likely

11. Supervisees can observe and learn from the supervisor, both directly and as a role model

12. Development of confidence and skills in groups may be transferable to work with service users

13. Allows a gradual step from dependence on the supervisor, through a lesser dependence on peers, to self-dependence

14. Allows greater empowerment through lateral teaching, learning, and support of peers (Brown & Bourne, 1996, p. 162)

Disadvantages

1. To maintain relevance of discussions to the widest numbers, specific and urgent needs are often only discussed in generalized terms

2. The group may stimulate sibling rivalry and peer competition that hinder the supervisory process

3. It is more difficult to incorporate a new appointee into a supervisory group than to provide them with individual supervision

4. It is easier to hide and opt out of the responsibility to engage in exploration, problem solving, and decision making

5. Greater opportunities for critical feedback, which can be inhibiting if confidence is lacking

6. The supervisor is more exposed and requires greater self-assurance than in individual supervision

7. Communication and interventions that assist one member may create problems for others

8. While encouraging autonomy, the supervisor may find it more difficult to restore the focus should the group follow a non-productive route

9. Supervisors will have to acquire or refresh their knowledge of group interaction, group dynamics, and individual behavior in the group context

10. The supervisor must focus both on the individual and the group

11. In highly cohesive groups, the pressure to conform to group thinking and attitudes can become counterproductive (Brown & Bourne, 1996, p. 162)

In sum, group supervision is a supplementary, and sometimes a complementary, format to the widely used individual supervision. However, it may require both supervisors and supervisees to open themselves up before they can benefit from the supervisory process.

9

Planning and Preparation

This chapter examines the preparation for and technical arrangements of supervision sessions. While it may appear that such basic arrangements can be taken for granted, insufficient or ill-conceived preparation can jeopardize the goals of social work supervision. Preparatory arrangements include the physical setting, the supervisory contract, the agenda and record, the duration and frequency, the content of discussion, and other considerations and constraints.

THE PHYSICAL SETTING

The physical context of social work supervision, including the location and the seating plan, was discussed in Chapter 4. The four Cs of a successful physical setting are comfort, confidentiality, communication, and compatibility. Comfort is achieved when both parties enjoy talking and expressing their feelings in the physical setting. The physical setting should be designed to make them feel natural and at home. A comfortable setting enhances a sense of security, which encourages the parties to exchange views. The elements of a comfortable physical setting include appropriate temperature and humidity, an absence of background noise, and enough private space.

Confidentiality refers to an acceptable level of privacy. The physical arrangement should ensure the security of information about clients in order to allow the supervisor and the supervisee to discuss sensitive professional, personnel, and even personal issues. A physical setting that provides a sense of confidentiality is a reflection of the values represented in the professional code of ethics of social workers. In supervision sessions, the discussion of a client's situation is strictly for the purpose of ensuring and improving quality of service to the client. In human service organizations, there are also organizational policies and procedures for ensuring the confidentiality of the client's information. When discussing sensitive matters related to colleagues, confidentiality is not only a must, but also a moral commitment, as it protects and respects fellow workers. Finally, when personal matters are discussed, confidentiality ensures the privacy of the supervisee. This may encourage frontline staff to express their own feelings.

Communication refers to a clear and open exchange of information and feelings between the supervisor and the supervisee, which is enhanced by an appropriate physical setting. During the supervision session, there should be no disturbances from telephone calls or other staff. This allows the supervisor and the supervisee to be focused.

Compatibility is achieved when the physical setting reflects the organizational goals, structure, processes, and culture. Because supervision is a part of an organizational system, it must conform to organizational objectives. For example, the leader of an outreach team for young people with behavioral problems stated that he usually invites his staff to open areas to have casual and informal discussions. He does so because the general director of the organization prefers this style of supervision. The organizational culture has a strong influence on the format of supervision, even in terms of the arrangement of the physical setting.

THE CONTRACT

Before the first session of social work supervision, a contract, either verbal or written, should be established. Without the contract, the expectations, boundaries, and objectives of the supervisor will differ from those of the supervisee. Because negotiating these differences would be very difficult within supervision sessions, they should be settled before the supervisory process starts. According to Powell (1993), a contract provides realistic tasks for both the supervisor and the supervisee, and reassures anxious supervisees by limiting their responsibilities. Several objectives must be fulfilled in order to establish a successful teaching relationship: establishing trust and respect; assessing the supervisee's practice knowledge and skills, experiences, and training needs; agreeing to a behavioral contract establishing the ground rules for the supervisory sessions; and setting learning goals. In addition, the supervisor must become familiar with the knowledge base, learning style, conceptual skills, suitability for work setting, and motivation of the supervisee.

Brown and Bourne (1996) maintained that a supervisory contract should take into account nine elements: the nature of the relationship, the format of supervision, accountability, focus, scheduling, confidentiality, agenda setting and record keeping, values, and evaluation. According to Osborne and Davis (1996), the contract must address six issues: the objectives of supervision, the context of services, the method of evaluation, duties and responsibilities, procedural considerations, and the supervisor's scope of practice. Fox (1983) suggested that goal setting in supervision is most effective when the goals are specific, explicit, feasible, realistic, attainable, constraint sensitive, relevant to the task formulated, modifiable, and prioritized. He proposed a goal-focused supervisory contract that reflects a mature and professional attitude; a firm knowledge base; rational decision making; a fundamental understanding and assessment of needs, and an awareness of learning motivation, shared responsibilities, the bases of competence evaluation, and the necessity of developing independent skills.

To match the unique needs of the supervisee with the knowledge and skills of the supervisor, Fox (1983, p. 39) suggested that both parties answer the following questions: What do we expect from each other? What can we give to each other? Are our goals the same? How can we achieve them? What constraints exist? How do we know when we have achieved the goals?

A closer examination of these questions is illuminating.

What Do We Expect From Each Other?

Before the first supervision session, the supervisor and the supervisee should state their expectations of each other. These expectations will be the foundation of the cooperation and consensus necessary in the supervisory process. Clarification of the expectations should be as specific as possible. Before discussing expectations, however, the supervisor and the supervisee may wish to discuss the values and experiences that have shaped these expectations. The supervisor should take the initiative to be open and frank in this discussion. This will pave the way for the supervisee and increase the probability of useful self-disclosure. It is also a good ice-breaking strategy. After the supervisor and the supervisee share their beliefs and experiences, the parties will find it easier to express their expectations of future supervision sessions. The supervisor should not push the supervisee to be frank, however. For some supervisees, it takes time to build up confidence in a supervisor.

What Can We Give to Each Other?

The supervisor and the supervisee should understand that there is a "give and take" dynamic in the supervisory process. Supervision should never be a one-way process. A supervision session is not just a briefing session or a reporting session. Both parties have the responsibility to contribute and the right to learn. This "horizontal" perspective departs from the traditional hierarchical view that the supervisee is always accountable to the supervisor. In the horizontal relationship of professional peers, both the supervisor and the supervisee must be prepared to exchange views. This exchange includes their experiences, ideas, and concerns. In the process, there is close interpersonal interaction, providing a foundation for the supervisory relationship.

Are Our Goals the Same?

Supervision cannot proceed successfully and smoothly without clearly defined and mutually agreed-upon goals. The direction of supervision, in fact, serves as an important guideline for professional development, not only for supervisees but also for supervisors (if they wish to supervise effectively). Consensus between the supervisor and the supervisee also ensures that clients will benefit from consistent, goal-directed intervention. If the supervisor and the supervisee find that their goals differ, they must discuss these differences openly. Both should adopt an inclusive attitude and search for a common ground to develop a consensus (not merely a compromise) that does not threaten their individual points of view.

How Can We Achieve Them?

Agreeing upon the direction of the supervision sessions is not sufficient to ensure their success. A step-by-step "how-to" program is also indispensable. This program should outline the format of supervision, the duration and frequency of supervision sessions, the preparation required, the use of time during the supervision sessions, and the roles of the supervisor and the supervisee. As Brown and Bourne (1996) pointed out, arrangements regarding the duration, frequency, and flexibility of supervision may seem to be technical details, but their effects can be critical. The most important element is to schedule supervision sessions at regular intervals. Supervisees should also understand that their supervisor is always available if they are in need. This understanding provides a sense of security and professional support. It also enhances the confidence of the frontline social workers in the process of intervention. Regularly scheduled supervision sessions reflect the supervisor's commitment to the professional development of the supervisee on a continual, rather than crisis intervention or ad hoc, basis. Once the schedule of the supervision session is made, it should be maintained.

What Constraints Exist?

It is important to be realistic in supervisory practice. Supervision does not occur in a vacuum; it occurs in an organizational context. All social workers, supervisors and frontline social workers alike, face various constraints. Some are imposed by the organization, for example, lack of resources. Others may be imposed by the task environment (e.g., the keen competition among different human service organizations). Although we may not be able to eliminate these constraints, we can identify them and respond with a more realistic and, therefore, more effective approach in the process of supervision.

How Will We Know When We Have Achieved the Goals?

After the goals are set, the supervisor and the supervisee need to establish yardsticks for goal achievement. Regular review of their achievement should be made on the basis of the process of interventions. After the evaluation, the supervisor should draw attention to measures for improvement.

In some cultures, the supervisor and the supervisee will not feel comfortable with a written supervisory contract because they will view it as an indication of mutual distrust. In this situation, a verbal agreement may serve as the contract. It should establish the objectives, expectations, rights, responsibilities, format, duration, and frequency of the supervision sessions. This agreement is very important, because it builds systematic planning into the supervisory process. Often when the agreement is drafted by supervisees, their sense of autonomy and their motivation increase. Because the relationship is a partnership, the supervisor should have the opportunity to add items to the agreement. However, the supervisor should not delete any items without the consent of the supervisee. This protects the right of the supervisees to raise any item of concern.

In the United States, supervisory contracts are used to establish an explicit and direct statement of the purposes, functions, and format of supervisory practice. The need to establish a clear, goal-oriented contract between the supervisor and the supervisee is emphasized in the American literature on supervision (Fox, 1983; Kaiser, 1997; Munson, 2002). As Kaiser (1997) explained, a supervisory contract creates mutual understanding, obtains cooperation to work on the client's problem, and determines the criteria for evaluation in order to establish shared meanings between the supervisor and the supervisee. Fox (1983) emphasized that the supervisory contract may also protect the independence of the supervisee in an unequal power relationship by clarifying potential sources of disagreement. Both Fox (1983) and Kaiser (1997) provided clear frameworks and guidelines for developing a supervisory contract. A supervisory contract should include information about the supervision's structure, process, standards, confidentiality, priorities, and feedback system.

Some supervisors in the United States use a specific "sessional contract" (Shulman, 1993) in addition to the general supervisory contract. The sessional contract delineates the tasks to be completed before the next supervision session. Although these contracts are rarely put into writing, they are clearly understood by both parties (Munson, 2002). In the supervisory contract, the frequency, length, and scheduling of sessions, as well as the learning method, are clearly stated (Kaiser, 1997). Granvold (1978a, 1978b) found that supervision in North America includes regular, formal conferences; written communication with supervisees; reviews of agency effectiveness through follow-up records; and implementation of time studies. Of course, these measures may be used by supervisors as institutional means to control their staff; however, because the duties and practice approach are usually well defined by the organizations, the supervisor may not interfere with the direct practice of frontline social workers. Such interference would make the supervisory process and supervisory relationship less personal.

Agency policy, the nature of the service setting, the tasks, and the experience and attitude of the supervisees influence the format and frequency of social work supervision. For example, in a residential setting, the staff are on shift duty, so it is difficult to bring everyone together for a group supervision session. Still, the unit needs to hold such sessions in order to discuss issues that affect everyone in the residential unit. Arrangements must be made so that every staff member can attend a weekly session. In another setting, seniority of staff may be a crucial factor in determining the format of supervision. Carrie, who is in charge of a children and youth center, told me that she considers factors such as the seniority, personality, and gender of the staff when deciding on the supervision format.

Carrie said, "There are different foci for different staff according to their personality and gender. For staff with strong personalities, a non-directive method will be adopted. As a woman, it is easier to talk with another woman; for example, it is easy to have physical contact. As a woman, supervising a male subordinate is difficult. The male supervisee feels it is difficult to agree with what a female supervisor says. The older staff also question a supervisor's method of conducting the supervision session. When dealing with these situations, I ask my supervisor for help."

AGENDAS AND RECORDS

An agenda is a contract for a specific supervision session. It lists the theme for discussion. This arrangement achieves a greater balance of power between the supervisor and the supervisee; it safeguards the autonomy of the supervisee while retaining supervisory authority.

For their records, both parties can jot down notes if they wish. The notes serve as a record for administrative purposes, a commitment to professional development, or a draft for follow-up actions. Notes can contain administrative instructions, professional advice, or requests to attend staff development programs. In addition, notes contain valuable information for performance appraisals. However, the supervisor and the supervisee should not devote the session to the evaluation of job performance; the atmosphere of the supervision session will become tense and political. Performance appraisal sessions should be conducted elsewhere. The supervisor should not jot down notes when supervisees mention their errors, weaknesses, and personal difficulties. Supervisees should be encouraged to freely express their feelings.

The agenda for a supervision session may follow the pattern outlined below:

1. Sharing feelings about work
   a. By the supervisor
   b. By the supervisee

2. Administrative report
   Coffee break

3. Focused discussion on practice-related issues

4. Any other business

It is recommended that the supervisor make some notes for the record. Supervisees should also be encouraged to write a one-page report of the session. During the writing process, the supervisee will reflect on the discussion. This reduces the workload of the supervisor and heightens the supervisee's sense of security. Of course, the report should be passed to the supervisor for endorsement and recording. The supervisor should have an opportunity to add comments if necessary.

DURATION AND FREQUENCY

The time factors, including the duration, frequency, and flexibility, of supervision sessions may seem to be simple technical issues that can be easily handled. These factors, however, often affect the development and quality of the supervisory relationship. Brown and Bourne (1996) suggested that the full duration of the interview should be firmly maintained. If there is nothing to talk about in a supervision session, there may be a lack of mutual trust. This is sometimes considered "good enough" supervision. However, if such sessions continue, they reflect problems in the structure or format of supervision. The "doorknob syndrome" (when a supervisee raises a very important issue during the last minute of the supervision session) indicates a problem in setting the priorities for discussion and possibly a lack of effective communication between the supervisor and the supervisee. In such cases, it is not advisable to extend the supervision session in a casual manner; instead, it is time to review the duration and frequency of the supervision session and look into the supervisory relationship.

The optimal duration of an individual session is one and one-half hours. The first 15 minutes can be spent sharing feelings about the job. The supervisor should take the initiative and set an example of openness. There is no need for full disclosure, but the ideas and facts that are discussed must be true (or at least, believed to be true). After creating a congenial atmosphere and establishing an understanding of each other's emotional state, the participants may spend half an hour discussing administrative matters. This discussion should be confined to those items that cannot be easily addressed in other meetings. At this point in the session, a five-minute break provides an opportunity to drink a cup of coffee or answer telephone calls. This break is necessary because the normal attention span of human beings is about 45 minutes. After the break, the last 40 minutes of the session may be spent in a discussion of social work values, professional knowledge, and practice skills related to intervention. The topic of discussion should be decided upon by the supervisor and the supervisee in advance so that both parties have the opportunity to collect relevant information. The discussion should enable the supervisor to identify training needs. If the supervisor cannot solve practice problems in the supervision session, it may be necessary to invite an external expert to provide some on-the-job training, not only for the supervisee but also for other members of the staff with similar training needs.

Brown and Bourne (1996) maintained that supervision sessions must be regular and reliable. This routine allows the supervisee to feel secure and comfortable. Human beings will only open their minds to change, growth, and development when they feel secure. Social workers are no exception. The frequency of the sessions depends on the needs of the parties involved: the supervisee, the supervisor, the agency, and the client. It should take into account the training needs of the supervisee, the assessment performed by the supervisor, the requirements of the agency, and the urgency of the client's problems. There is no golden rule. Often, a monthly team meeting and individual meetings every two weeks in the clinical practice setting are adequate. Of course, it is necessary for the supervisor to increase the number of sessions if the staff are inexperienced or there are problems with job performance. Payne (1994) found that newly qualified staff receive more frequent and more challenging supervision than experienced staff.

THE CONTENT OF DISCUSSION

Traditionally, the content of the discussion in supervision sessions includes administrative and educational matters. The session should begin with a supportive discussion. A supportive atmosphere encourages the supervisee to be receptive and communicative. After the supervisor's opening remarks, the supervisee may respond by discussing his or her feelings about the work content or context. A medical social worker at a large public hospital said, "What I consult my supervisor about is all related to agency policy. For matters related to my clients, I only seek advice when there is trouble. When we can also talk about our feelings, the results of supervision are much better." A youth worker with six years of experience in children and youth services expressed her feelings about supervision: "Usually we have time to talk about our feelings. Every time, I really feel that I am talking with a friend. However, I also remind myself to be rational. She is my boss. I am reserved about some things, especially when my views on the programs do not match hers."

In practice, there are different foci of discussion depending on the staff. As the manager of a children and youth center explained, "There are different foci for different staff according to their seniority, personality, and gender. For junior staff, supervision is orientation. For experienced staff, supervision is training and development. For staff with strong personalities, a non-directive method will be adopted." As an experienced school social work supervisor observed, "For new staff, the most important thing is to calm them down. I don't handle administrative matters in supervision sessions. I help them to handle relationships with high-school teachers and the dynamics in the school. After that, I ask them to draft a service plan. As a supervisor, my duty is to help the staff recognize their strengths and weaknesses, position themselves in a team, and survive and function in a service agency. Emotional support is very important to both new and experienced staff."

During the administrative part of the supervision session, the discussion should focus on sensitive matters that relate to the supervisee and that should not be handled in staff meetings or program planning meetings. To discuss all administrative tasks in detail during the session is not an effective or efficient supervisory practice. The discussion in the session should be limited to that which requires face-to-face discussion between the supervisor and the supervisee (for example, the critical problems of the client in a counseling case). Daily contact, memos, and meetings can serve as mechanisms for handling routine administrative tasks. There is no need to discuss them in supervision sessions. The session is a good time to make joint decisions on matters related to professional practice that are particularly related to the supervisee. If this principle is maintained, half an hour will usually suffice. Some supervisors choose to discuss the direction and principles of intervention instead of the details of every case. As a highly experienced supervisor of a counseling center explained, "I think the most important aspects of supervision are the ethics and principles involved in handling cases, not micro practice skills."

A discussion that is focused on practice issues fulfills an educational function. Topics should be suggested by the supervisee and sanctioned by the supervisor well in advance of the session. This allows the supervisor and the supervisee ample time for information collection and preparation. If the supervisor is not familiar with an issue, he or she may consult external experts. When several supervisees suggest the same topic for focused discussion, a group session for staff development may be organized.

CONSIDERATIONS AND CONSTRAINTS

Establishing the boundaries of supervision sessions is very important. As Brown and Bourne (1996) asked, "What is not the appropriate business of supervision?" This issue must be addressed at the very beginning, that is, at the time the contract is formed. The supervisor and the supervisee must have a basic understanding of what belongs within the supervision session and what belongs elsewhere. The discussion of boundaries should take into account a number of factors: seniority, expertise, emotional state, gender, and flexibility. The basic principles in setting these boundaries are to understand the differences, respect diversity, and achieve a consensus between the supervisor and the supervisee.

Finally, we have to remember that the supervision process must be creative, engaging, enabling, and ensuring (Brown & Bourne, 1996). New ideas should be encouraged and acknowledged. Both the supervisor and the supervisee can learn and grow. Supervision should also be a process that makes supervisees feel that they belong in an organization. The staff should feel that they are directly engaged with their client and with the organization. Supervision offers supervisees an opportunity to reflect upon their practice and attempt to actualize their ideals. Finally, the effect of supervision should be long lasting. It has a great impact on the direct practice of the supervisee.

As Brown and Bourne (1996) pointed out, supervision is a time-out, a safe haven, and an opportunity to take stock. It is also a time for exploration, reflection, learning, and problem solving. Effective supervision will benefit the worker personally and also improve relationships with clients, collaboration within the team, and the ability to work toward agency goals. The process is beneficial not only to the supervisee and the client but also to the supervisor.

10

The State of the Art of Research on Social Work Supervision

A REVIEW OF RESEARCH STUDIES

As noted earlier, supervision has come to occupy a unique and important position in social work practice. It is recognized as the primary factor in determining the quality of service to clients and the level of professional development and job satisfaction of social workers (Harkness, 1995; Harkness & Hensley, 1991; Harkness & Poertner, 1989; Kadushin & Harkness, 2002). However, there is a dearth of empirical research literature on the actual practice of supervision (Erera & Lazar, 1994a; Harkness & Poertner, 1989; Loganbill, Hardy, & Delworth, 1982; Tsui, 1997b). Unlike student fieldwork supervision, where the types and extent of supervision can be readily examined for research purposes, staff supervision in social work—which is embedded in an organizational context—cannot be so easily investigated. Due to the hierarchical power relationship between the supervisor and the supervisee and to the confidential nature of the process, it is an extremely delicate and difficult task to elicit information about the supervisory performance of a supervisor or a supervisee within an organizational setting. These difficulties may account for the fact that there are fewer empirical studies on staff supervision than on student supervision in the field of social work.

CRITERIA FOR SELECTING
EMPIRICAL RESEARCH LITERATURE

All the empirical research literature published between 1950 and 2002 on staff supervision of social workers was reviewed for this study. Altogether, 34 pieces of research were identified. Five criteria were used to identify the relevant literature. First, selection was limited to literature published in refereed journals or books. Second, the literature was confined to that published between 1950 and 2002. No database or back-dated issues of professional journals in social work could be found before 1950. Third, it was necessary that the focus of the research be related to supervision for social workers in human service organizations. Fourth, only empirical studies that collected firsthand information were included. Theoretical discussions on supervision were not considered. Fifth, in cases where authors published similar results and discussions from a single research project in various academic journals, only the most influential and significantly cited article was selected for review.

Selection Procedures

As a result of the above-mentioned selection criteria, the research came from three major sources (for the full list of the research literature, see the Appendix). First, all the entries under the key word "supervision" from electronic databases, such as Social Work Abstracts, PsycLIT, and Sociology, were scanned. Second, all the articles published in the major journal on supervision, *The Clinical Supervisor* (founded in 1983), were scanned. Finally, the bibliographies of the updated versions of the two most popular and comprehensive texts on supervision, Kadushin and Harkness's (2002) *Supervision in Social Work* (4th ed.) and Munson's (2002) *Handbook of Clinical Social Work Supervision* (3rd ed.), were scanned.

Researchers

In the 1970s, Kadushin (1974) conducted a large-scale national survey on social work supervision in the United States. The random sample was composed of 750 supervisors and 750 supervisees. This was the first attempt to provide a picture of social work supervision in the United States at a particular time. Munson (1976) published his doctoral dissertation on the uses of structural, authoritative, and teaching models in social work supervision. His empirical study involved 65 dyads of social work supervisors and supervisees. The results were published several times (Munson, 1976, 1979a, 1979b, 1981). After this period, research on social work supervision began to be published with increasing frequency.

Shulman, Robinson, and Luckj (1981) conducted a wide-ranging survey of the context and the skills of social work supervision. It remains the most comprehensive survey undertaken in Canada. Following the path of Kadushin (1974, 1992b, 1992c), Munson (1976, 1979a, 1979b, 1981), and Shulman and colleagues (Shulman, 1993; Shulman et al., 1981), a number of younger scholars conducted significant research studies on a variety of supervisory issues in the 1980s and 1990s (see, e.g., Eisikovitz, Meier, Guttman, Shurka, & Levinstein, 1985; Erera & Lazar, 1993, 1994a, 1994b; Harkness, 1995, 1997; Harkness & Hensley, 1991; Harkness & Poertner, 1989; Poertner & Rapp, 1983; York & Denton, 1990; York & Hastings, 1985). Some of these studies borrowed from the frameworks established by Kadushin (1976, 1985, 1992a), Munson (1993, 2002), and Shulman and colleagues (Shulman, 1993; Shulman et al., 1981). For example, Erera and Lazar (1994b) operationalized Kadushin's model of supervision to create the Supervisory Functions Inventory and validated the model's utility as a measurement tool. Eisikovitz et al. (1985) adopted Munson's instrument for measuring the worker's evaluation of supervision in their study of supervision and work context. Harkness (1995, 1997) tested Shulman's interactional social work theory by examining the association among skills, relationships, and outcomes in supervised social work practice.

Research Focus

The 34 research studies published in the past 50 years can be divided into three categories, according to their focus of research: basic descriptive studies, studies on supervisory issues, and studies on client outcomes. In the studies on supervisory issues, eight issues emerge as significant concerns for researchers: supervisory functions; the supervisory context; structure and authority; the supervisory relationship; supervisory style and skills; job satisfaction; training for supervisors; and gender issues.

CRITIQUE OF EXISTING RESEARCH
LITERATURE ON SOCIAL WORK SUPERVISION

The following is a critical review of the research methodology used in the empirical studies outlined above; it addresses their research subjects, sampling methods, research designs, modes of data collection, and data analyses.

Research Subjects

Nearly half of the studies (16 out of 34) involved both the supervisor and the supervisee (e.g., Harkness, 1997; Kadushin, 1974, 1992b, 1992c; Ko, 1987; Munson, 1979a, 1979b; Shulman et al., 1981). Eight studies focused on the supervisor (e.g., Erera & Lazar, 1993, 1994a, 1994b; Granvold, 1977, 1978b), and nine, on the supervisee (e.g., Gray, 1990; Greenspan, Hanfling, Parker, Primm, & Waldfogel, 1991; Pilcher, 1984; Rauktis & Koeske, 1994). There was, however, scant research based on the pairing of the supervisor and the supervisee as a dyad, thus enabling the researcher to look at the interactive dynamics of the supervisory relationship. This kind of research design is difficult to achieve because there is a power differential between the supervisor and the supervisee and it is extremely difficult to find research subjects willing to participate in the study. As mentioned before, only Munson (1981) tried to pair supervisors with their supervisees in his study. Harkness and Hensley (1991) conducted the only study dealing with client outcomes, the ultimate goal of supervisory practice, and found that there was a pattern of associations among skills, relationships, and outcomes. In addition, Harkness (1995) designed an experiment that showed that mixed focused supervision produces better outcomes in terms of client satisfaction and general contentment.

Sampling Methods

More than half of the studies (19 out of 34) used random sampling methods, including cluster sampling, systematic sampling, and surveying the whole population. Among the 34 studies reviewed, only five used non-random sampling, while another seven administered questionnaires to all subjects. However, the response rates of some large-scale studies were not satisfactory. As Rubin and Babbie (1997) noted, a 70 percent response is required if one wants to generalize the findings. However, few research studies in social work supervision achieve this response rate.

Research Design

Many of the studies reviewed were exploratory. Often, they did not have a clearly stated hypothesis. A generalized conceptual definition of supervision was frequently used, making the construct of "supervision" too vague to operationalize and to test precisely. This omission affects the construct validity of the research design. Most of the studies were one-shot, cross-sectional surveys. Some of them were conducted on a large scale (e.g., Himle, Jayaratne, & Thyness, 1989; Kadushin, 1974, 1992b, 1992c; Shulman et al., 1981; Vinokur-Kaplan, 1987). There were only a few in-depth studies: Melichercik (1984) used self-administered diaries to collect information about the daily activities of supervisors over a period of one week; Harkness and his colleagues (1991, 1995) used an experiment to examine the impact of supervision; and Dendinger and Kohn (1989) reassessed a small portion of the samples of their study after six months in order to validate the Supervisory Skills Inventory (SSI).

Research Methods

There is a lack of longitudinal studies, particularly panel studies, which observe samples at different points in time. Quantitative methods were often adopted for analyzing the data, but in-depth qualitative research methods were seldom used. The lack of comprehensive and all-round research on social work supervision reflects the fact that empirical research on social work supervision is still in the stages of early development. Researchers still tend to focus their main efforts on providing an overview of supervisory issues in practice, rather than carrying out in-depth investigations aimed at theory construction or model development. There is a strong need for researchers to conduct qualitative studies that explore the functioning of social work supervision in various cultural contexts in order to build theoretical models of social work supervision.

RELEVANCE TO THEORY BUILDING

The limitations of research design mentioned above reflect the difficulties of conducting studies on social work supervision. It is very difficult to get the support of supervisors, supervisees, and human service organizations for research on this delicate issue. The majority of existing studies focus on issues in the supervisory process. They seldom focus on client outcomes, and only one study treats the supervisor and the supervisee as a dyad. Although a number of researchers have conducted studies on supervision during the last five decades, there has been a lack of programmatic investigation, particularly in the area of theory building. None of the studies discusses the impact of specific cultural contexts on social work supervision, although cultural traits may be a very important factor affecting the supervisory relationship. The review of the empirical research suggests that scholars should conduct qualitative research to review the research agenda for the future.

RESEARCH AGENDA FOR THE FUTURE

Supervision has long been recognized as an organizational practice (Holloway & Brager, 1989; Miller, 1987; Munson, 2002). When supervision is viewed more comprehensively as an interactional process involving four parties (i.e., the human service organization, the supervisor, the frontline worker, and the client) in a societal culture, we need to identify the factors that affect all four participating parties. There is a critical need for researchers to study supervision in specific cultural contexts, both societal and organizational.

As supervision aims to ensure and enhance the quality of service to clients, it is important to look into the relationship between different models and formats of supervision and their impact on worker job performance and client outcomes (Tsui, 1998a). Harkness and Poertner (1989) proposed a reconceptualization of research on supervision. They suggested using multiple definitions of social work supervision, various service strategies related to supervisory practice, and multiple linkages between supervisory practice and client outcomes in a range of service settings. In this research model, the assessment of effectiveness of supervisory practice would include measures applied to multiple sources (i.e., supervisor, worker, client, and agency).

In human service organizations, supervision can be taken as a form of knowledge management. Knowledge management is an essential element of staff development. It refers to an organization's capacity to educate staff and to be educated by staff as well as clients (Quinn, Anderson, & Finkelstein, 1998). Supervisors who work with frontline workers to gather, use, and share information about their clients and services can make better decisions regarding program development. Through this process, frontline workers can see how their talent, knowledge, and experiences contribute to the improvement of service delivery and client outcomes. It is also useful to identify how the roles and functions of supervision complement other kinds of staff development. For example, the training functions of supervision in the commercial sector are often supplemented by consultation and mentoring.

Over the last five decades, researchers have identified the nature of supervision but not what supervision should be. The studies help to describe the reality, but they do not prescribe the ideal. To realize the dreams of supervisors and supervisees for supervision, it is necessary to ask the following research questions: (a) How do supervisors use their authority to ensure effective job performance and motivation of their staff? (b) What are the core supervisory practices needed to handle the wide range of issues in supervisory relationships? (c) What are specific and concrete guidelines for conducting supervisory sessions? (d) What are the different stages of development of the supervisory process experienced by supervisors and frontline workers? (e) What are the practices that have proven to be effective in handling difficult issues in supervisory practice? (Tsui, 2004)

FROM THE REALITY TO THE IDEAL

This book traced the roots of supervisory practice, examined supervisory theories, and explored the specific features of social work supervision. All these efforts contribute to an understanding of the nature of social work supervision. The experience of writing this book revealed that, although the functions of social work supervision are influenced by the contexts of supervisory practice, the ideal of social work supervision can be jointly shaped by the supervisor and the supervisee.

Many supervisees, especially young ones, hope that they will receive supervision that has the same format as the student fieldwork supervision that they received during their years of social work training. Supervisees hope that the supervision sessions will be regular and that dates and times for supervision sessions will be fixed in advance, so that both parties can prepare for them. The content of supervision sessions should be comprehensive, and cover policy, practice, and skills. Most of the time in supervision sessions should be spent discussing work, and part of it should be focused on sharing ideas and feelings. Job requirements should be described and explained in concrete terms. Supervisees do not mind high standards and strict requirements, but they need clear direction and specific, action-oriented guidelines. If they achieve their goals, they expect their supervisor's appreciation and recognition. When they make mistakes, they welcome their supervisor's view of what went wrong, if it is expressed in a friendly manner. However, supervisors tend to give vague advice, which is not action oriented. Supervisors learn supervisory practice from their supervisors and follow the same pattern. The quality of social work supervision directly and significantly affects the quality of direct service to clients, as well as the morale and commitment of staff social workers (Tsui, 2001).

Supervisors hope that supervision can be individualized and tailor-made for supervisees. There should be no use of administrative authority. The highest level of supervision is to have nothing to supervise (in keeping with the Taoist belief in the value of nothingness that is integral to traditional Chinese culture). Good supervision should enhance the professional growth of the staff by identifying their strengths and weaknesses, and should provide resources and opportunities for improvement, in order to achieve service accountability. This approach would benefit the supervisor, the supervisee, and the clients. Good supervision should also lead to the establishment of a trusting relationship between the supervisor and the supervisee. Agreement between the supervisor and the supervisee should be achieved for decision making, and participation should be encouraged. Supervisees require support, encouragement, and empathy. Eventually, the staff's sense of belonging to the organization will increase. If the sessions are arranged regularly with an advance schedule, the supervisor and the supervisee will be well prepared. Locations other than the supervisor's office should sometimes be used for supervision sessions. The supervisor should serve as a role model for the supervisee.

From the supervisee's perspective, ideal supervision is focused more on the affective side. This is because the supervisor-supervisee relationship is a personal one-on-one relationship for supervisees. They hope that supervision will be a natural and comfortable sharing process in which there is two-way communication, along with flexibility and recognition. The supervisor should be human, fair, and empathetic. Ideal supervision should also serve as an opportunity for reflection.

The supervisor should enable the supervisee to become a competent professional practitioner. Advice must be specific, clear, and concrete. Supervisors should provide insights from their "super-vision."

SOCIAL WORK SUPERVISION: A PERSONAL REFLECTION

If social workers were asked to identify a unique characteristic of their profession, the practice of supervision would be a likely choice. Social work supervision is one of the major mechanisms of monitoring the quality of service and a tool for the development of professional social workers. Of course, this book does not bring the effort of knowledge building to an end; it is a starting point for a new journey on the part of researchers, educators, and practitioners.

Writing a book is, by nature, a lonely process. The long journey of writing this book has made me more empathetic to the supervisor— "a marginal person" mediating between top management and frontline staff. There are demands and deadlines to meet, but few opportunities to share difficulties and frustrations. Thus, peer support is very important to both supervisors and researchers. During the writing process, I was very lucky to have academic peers who were interested in my work and give me advice.

It was necessary to blend my two roles—as an experienced supervisor and as a teacher of a postgraduate course on supervision—in the writing process. The change of identity from "supervisor" to "teacher of supervisors" and then to "writer on supervision" has been difficult to negotiate alone. This journey involves interactions and struggle among the personal self, the professional self, and the academic self. In this book, I discovered that I had used my "self" to explore supervisory practice. I often reminded myself that I must put my professional self aside and try to be more academic. However, without my professional self, I would not have been able to interpret the rich practice experience. When I reviewed the literature about supportive functions of supervision, my personal self reminded me that it is necessary to share what I believe.

Supervision makes social work practice not only effective and efficient but also unique and human. Therefore, it is important for us to revisit the nature and essence of social work before we embark on supervisory practice. When we practice supervision, we have to be both culturally sensitive and contextually specific. We have to remember that we, too, are social workers. As supervisors, we should see supervisees not only as staff members but also as human beings with motives and dignity. Supervision is not merely a mechanism for ensuring service accountability; it is also an opportunity to pursue personal and professional growth. During this long journey of exploration, I reconfirmed my belief that to be natural and human is the ultimate and universal principle for supervisory practice and social work intervention.

Appendix

A List of Empirical
Research on Staff Supervision
in Social Work (1950–2002)

Dendinger, D. C., & Kohn, E. (1989). Assessing supervisory skills. *The Clinical Supervisor, 7*(1), 41–55.

Eisikovitz, Z., Meier, R., Guttman, E., Shurka, E., & Levinstein, A. (1985). Supervision in ecological context: The relationship between the quality of supervision and the work and treatment environment. *Journal of Social Service Research, 8*(4), 37–58.

Erera, I. P., & Lazar, A. (1993). Training needs of social work supervisors. *The Clinical Supervisor, 11*(1), 83–93.

Erera, I. P., & Lazar, A. (1994a). The administrative and educational functions in supervision: Indications of incompatibility. *The Clinical Supervisor, 12*(2), 39–56.

Erera, I. P., & Lazar, A. (1994b). Operating Kadushin's model of social work supervision. *Journal of Social Service Research, 18*(3/4), 109–122.

Gibelman, M., & Schervish, P. H. (1997). Supervision in social work: Characteristics and trends in a changing environment. *The Clinical Supervisor, 16*(2), 1–15.

Granvold, D. K. (1977). Supervisory style and educational preparation of public welfare supervisors. *Administration in Social Work, 1*(1), 79–88.

Granvold, D. K. (1978). Training social work supervisors to meet organizational and worker objectives. *Journal of Education for Social Work, 14*(2), 38–45.

Gray, S. W. (1990). The interplay of social work and supervision: An exploratory study. *The Clinical Supervisor, 8*(1), 53–65.

Greenspan, R., Hanfling, S., Parker, E., Primm, S., & Waldfogel, D. (1991). Supervision of experienced agency workers: A descriptive study. *The Clinical Supervisor, 9*(2), 31–42.

Harkness, D. (1995). The art of helping in supervised practice: Skills, relationships, and outcomes. *The Clinical Supervisor, 13*(1), 63–76.

Harkness, D. (1997). Testing interactional social work theory: A panel analysis of supervised practice and outcomes. *The Clinical Supervisor, 15*(1), 33–50.

Harkness, D., & Hensley, H. (1991). Changing the focus of social work supervision: Effects on client satisfaction and generalized contentment. *Social Work, 37,* 506–512.

Himle, D. P., Jayaratne, S., & Thyness, P. A. (1989). The buffering effects of four types of supervisory support on work stress. *Administration in Social Work, 13*(1), 19–34.

Kadushin, A. (1974). Supervisor-supervisee: A survey. *Social Work, 19*(3), 288–298.

Kadushin, A. (1992b). Social work supervision: An updated survey. *The Clinical Supervisor, 10*(2), 9–27.

Kadushin, A. (1992c). What's wrong, what's right with social work supervision? *The Clinical Supervisor, 10*(1), 3–19.

Ko, G. P. (1987). Casework supervision in voluntary family service agencies in Hong Kong. *International Social Work, 30,* 171–184.

Melichercik, J. (1984). Social work supervision in transition: An exploration of current supervisory practice. *The Social Worker, 52*(3), 108–112.

Munson, C. E. (1979c). Evaluation of male and female supervisors. *Social Work, 24,* 104–110.

Munson, C. E. (1981). Style and structure in supervision. *Journal of Education for Social Work, 17*(1), 65–72.

Newsome, M., Jr., & Pillari, V. (1991). Job satisfaction and the worker-supervisor relationship. *The Clinical Supervisor, 9*(2), 119–129.

Pilcher, A. J. (1984). The state of social work supervision in Victoria according to the practitioners. *Australian Social Work, 37*(3/4), 33–43.

Poertner, J., & Rapp, C. (1983). What is social work supervision? *The Clinical Supervisor, 1*(2), 53–67.

Rauktis, M. E., & Koeske, G. F. (1994). Maintaining social worker morale: When supportive supervision is not enough. *Administration in Social Work, 18*(1), 39–60.

Russell, P. A., Lankford, M. W., & Grinnell, R. M. (1983). Attitudes toward supervisors in a human service agency. *The Clinical Supervisor, 1*(3), 57–71.

Scott, D., & Farrow, J. (1993). Evaluating standards of social work supervision in child welfare and hospital social work. *Australian Social Work, 46*(2), 33–41.

Scott, W. R. (1965). Reactions to supervision in a heteronomous professional organization. *Administrative Science Quarterly, 10,* 65–81.

Shulman, L. (1993). *Interactional supervision.* Washington, DC: NASW Press.

Shulman, L., Robinson, E., & Luckj, A. (1981). *A study of the content, context and skills of supervision.* Vancouver: University of British Columbia.

Vinokur-Kaplan, D. (1987). A national survey of in-service training experiences of child welfare supervisors and workers. *Social Service Review, 61*(2), 291–304.

Western New York Chapter, NASW Committee on Social Work. (1958). A chapter survey. *Social Work, 3,* 18–25.

York, R. O., & Denton, R. T. (1990). Leadership behavior and supervisory performance: The view from below. *The Clinical Supervisor, 8*(1), 93–108.

York, R. O., & Hastings, T. (1985). Worker maturity and supervisory leadership behavior. *Administration in Social Work, 9*(4), 37–46.

References

Abels, P. (1977). *The new practice of supervision and staff development: A synergistic approach.* New York: Association Press.

Abroms, G. M. (1977). Supervision as metatherapy. In F. W. Kaslow et al. (Eds.), *Supervision, consultation, and staff training in the helping professions* (pp. 81–99). San Francisco: Jossey-Bass.

Alonso, A. (1983). A developmental theory of psychodynamic supervision. *The Clinical Supervisor, 1*(3), 23–36.

Arches, J. (1991). Social structure, burnout, and job satisfaction. *Social Work, 36*(3), 202–206.

Arndt, H. C. M. (1955). Principles of supervision in public assistance agencies. *Social Casework, 36,* 307–313.

Atherton, J. S. (1986). *Professional supervision in group care: A contract-based approach.* London: Tavistock.

Austin, L. (1942). Supervision of the experienced caseworker. *The Family, 22*(9), 314–320.

Austin, L. (1952, December). Basic principles of supervision. *Social Casework,* 163–217.

Austin, L. (1956). An evaluation of supervision. *Social Casework, 37*(8), 375–382.

Austin, L. (1957). Supervision in social work. In R. H. Kurtz (Ed.), *Social work year book* (pp. 569–573). New York: National Association of Social Workers.

Austin, L. (1961). The changing role of the supervisor. *Smith College Studies in Social Work, 31*(3), 179–195.

Austin, M. J. (1981). *Supervisory management for the human services.* Englewood Cliffs, NJ: Prentice Hall.

Bacock, C. (1953, December). Social work as work. *Social Casework,* 415–422.

Barker, R. L. (1995). *Social work dictionary* (3rd ed.). Washington, DC: NASW Press.

Barnard, C. I. (1971). The theory of authority. In S. A. Yelaja (Ed.), *Authority and social work: Concept and use* (pp. 48–64). Toronto: University of Toronto Press.

Barretta-Herman, A. (1993). On the development of a model of supervision for licensed social work practitioners. *The Clinical Supervisor, 11*(2), 55–64.

Bennett, D. (1976). *TA and the manager.* New York: AMACOM.

Berkowitz, S. J. (1952). The administrative process in casework supervision. *Social Casework*, 419–423.

Bernard, C. I. (1968). *The functions of the executive.* Cambridge, MA: Harvard University Press.

Bernard, J. M. (1979). Supervisor training: A discrimination model. *Counselor Education and Supervision, 19,* 60–68.

Bernard, J. M., & Goodyear, R. K. (1992). *Fundamentals of clinical supervision.* Boston: Allyn & Bacon.

Bernardin, H. J. (1984). *Performance appraisal.* Belmont, CA: Kent.

Bernardin, H. J., & Beatty, R. W. (1987, Summer). Can subordinate appraisals enhance managerial productivity? *Sloan Management Review,* 63–73.

Berry, J. W., & Laponce, J. A. (Eds.). (1994). *Ethnicity and culture in Canada: The research landscape.* Toronto: University of Toronto Press.

Blumberg, M., & Pringle, C. D. (1982). The missing opportunity in organizational research: Some implications for a theory of work performance. *Academy of Management Review, 7*(4), 560–569.

Bogo, M. (1993). The student/field instructor relationship: The critical factor in field education. *The Clinical Supervisor, 11*(2), 23–36.

Bogo, M., & Vayda, E. (1988). *The practice of field instruction in social work.* Toronto: University of Toronto Press.

Bond, M. H. (1993). *Social psychology across cultures: Analysis and perspectives.* New York: Harvester Wheatsheaf.

Brashears, F. (1995). Supervision as social work practice: A reconceptualization. *Social Work, 40*(5), 692–699.

Brown, A., & Bourne, I. (1996). *The social work supervisor: Supervision in community, day care and residential settings.* Philadelphia: Open University Press.

Bruce, E. J., & Austin, M. J. (2000). Social work supervision: Assessing the past and mapping the future. *The Clinical Supervisor, 19*(2), 85–107.

Bunker, D. R., & Wijnberg, M. H. (1988). *Supervision and performance: Managing professional work in human service organizations.* San Francisco: Jossey-Bass.

Burns, C. I., & Holloway, E. L. (1989). Therapy in supervision: An unresolved issue. *The Clinical Supervisor, 7*(4), 47–60.

Burns, M. E. (1958). *The historical development of the process of casework supervision as seen in the professional literature of social work.* Unpublished doctoral dissertation, School of Social Work, University of Chicago.

Campbell, J. P., McHenry, J. J., & Wise, L. (1990). Modelling job performance in a population of jobs. *Personnel Psychology, 43,* 313–333.

Campion, M. A., & Goldfinch, J. R. (1981). Mentoring among hospital administrators. *Hospital and Health Services Administration, 26,* 77–93.

Chaiklin, H., & Munson, C. E. (1983). Peer consultation in social work. *The Clinical Supervisor, 1*(2), 21–34.

Chao, G. T. (1998). Invited reason: Challenging research in mentoring. *Human Resource Development Quarterly, 9*(4), 333–338.

Chau, K. (1995). Social work practice in a Chinese society: Reflections and challenges. *Hong Kong Journal of Social Work, 29*(2), 1–9.

Chernesky, R. H. (1986). A new model of supervision. In N. Van Den Bergh & L. B. Cooper (Eds.), *Feminist visions for social work* (pp. 128–148). Silver Spring, MD: National Association of Social Workers.

Cheung, F. C. H., & Tsui, M. S. (2002). A wake-up call to the social work profession. *Families in Society, 83*(2), 123–124.

Clarke, J., Gewirtz, S., & McLaughlin, E. (Eds.). (2000). *New managerialism, new welfare?* Thousand Oaks, CA: Sage.

Clarke, J., Gewirtz, S., & McLaughlin, E. (2001). New managerialism, new welfare? *The British Journal of Social Work, 31*(5), 818–820.

Clough, R. (1995). Making supervision work: Statutory and voluntary organizations. In J. Pritchard (Ed.), *Good practice in supervision* (pp. 99–111). London: Jessica Kingsley.

Cohen, B. (1987, May–June). The ethics of social work supervision revisited. *Social Work,* 194–196.

Cohen, N. A., & Rhodes, G. B. (1978). Social work supervision: A view toward leadership style and job orientation in education and practice. *Administration in Social Work, 1*(3), 281–291.

Collins, P. M. (1994). Does mentorship among social workers make a difference? An empirical investigation of career outcomes. *Social Work, 39*(4), 413–419.

Crespi, T. D. (1995). Gender sensitive supervision: Exploring feminist perspectives for male and female supervisors. *The Clinical Supervisor, 13*(2), 19–29.

Cummings, L. L., & Schwartz, D. P. (1973). *Performance in organizations: Determinants and appraisal.* Glenview, IL: Scott Foresman.

D'Andrade, R. G. (1984). Cultural meaning systems. In R. A. Shweder & R. A. LeVine (Eds.), *Culture theory: Essays on mind, self, and emotion* (pp. 88–119). Cambridge, UK: Cambridge University Press.

Dechert, C. (1965). Cybernetics and the human person. *International Philosophical Quarterly, 5,* 5–36.

Dendinger, D. C., & Kohn, E. (1989). Assessing supervisory skills. *The Clinical Supervisor, 7*(1), 41–55.

Devis, D. (1965). Teaching and administrative functions in supervision. *Social Work, 10*(2), 83–89.

Doehrman, M. J. G. (1976). *Parallel process in supervision.* Topeka, KS: Menninger Clinic.

Dublin, R. A. (1989). Supervision and leadership styles. *Social Casework: The Journal of Contemporary Social Work, 70*(10), 617–621.

Durry, S. S. (1984). *Assertive supervision: Building involved teamwork.* Champaign, IL: Research Press.

Eisenberg, S. S. (1956). Supervision as an agency need. *Social Casework, 37*(5), 23–37.

Eisikovitz, Z., & Guttman, E. (1983). Towards a practice theory of learning through experience in social work supervision. *The Clinical Supervisor, 1*(1), 51–63.

Eisikovitz, Z., Meier, R., Guttman, E., Shurka, E., & Levinstein, A. (1985). Supervision in ecological context: The relationship between the quality of supervision and the work and treatment environment. *Journal of Social Service Research, 8*(4), 37–58.

Encyclopedia of Social Work. (1965). Silver Spring, MD: National Association of Social Workers.

Encyclopedia of Social Work. (1971). Silver Spring, MD: National Association of Social Workers.

Encyclopedia of Social Work. (1977). Silver Spring, MD: National Association of Social Workers.

Encyclopedia of Social Work. (1987). Silver Spring, MD: National Association of Social Workers.

Encyclopedia of Social Work. (1995). Silver Spring, MD: National Association of Social Workers.

Enteman, W. F. (1993). *Managerialism: The emergence of a new ideology.* Madison, WI: University of Wisconsin Press.

Epstein, L. (1973). Is autonomous practice possible? *Social Work, 18,* 5–12.

Erera, I. P. (1991a). Role conflict among public welfare supervisors. *Administration in Social Work, 15*(4), 35–51.

Erera, I. P. (1991b). Supervisor can burn-out too. *The Clinical Supervisor, 9*(2), 131–148.

Erera, I. P., & Lazar, A. (1993). Training needs of social work supervisors. *The Clinical Supervisor, 11*(1), 83–93.

Erera, I. P., & Lazar, A. (1994a). The administrative and educational functions in supervision: Indications of incompatibility. *The Clinical Supervisor, 12*(2), 39–56.

Erera, I. P., & Lazar, A. (1994b). Operating Kadushin's model of social work supervision. *Journal of Social Service Research, 18*(3/4), 109–122.

Etzioni, A. (1969). *The semi-professions and their organization.* New York: Free Press.

Feldman, Y. (1950). The teaching aspect of casework supervision. *Social Casework, 31*(4), 156–161.

Fizadle, R. (1979). Peer-group supervision. In C. E. Munson (Ed.), *Social work supervision: Classic statements and critical issues* (pp. 122–132). New York: Free Press.

Flynn, N. (2000). Managerialism and public services: Some international trends. In J. Clarke, S. Gewirtz, & E. McLaughlin (Eds.), *New managerialism, new welfare?* (pp. 27–44). Thousand Oaks, CA: Sage.

Fox, R. (1983). Contracting in supervision: A goal oriented process. *The Clinical Supervisor, 1,* 37–49.

Fox, R. (1989). Relationship: The cornerstone of clinical supervision. *Social Casework, 70,* 146–152.

French, J. R. P., & Raven, B. (1960). The bases of social power. In D. Cartwright & A. Zander (Eds.), *Group dynamics* (pp. 607–623). Evanston, IL: Row, Peterson.

Galt, A., & Smith, L. (1976). *Models and the study of social change.* New York: Wiley.

Gardiner, D. (1989). *The anatomy of supervision: Developing learning and professional_competence for social work students.* London: Society for Research into Higher Education and Open University Press.

Garrett, K. J., & Barretta-Herman, A. (1995). Moving from supervision to professional development. *The Clinical Supervisor, 13*(2), 97–110.

Getzel, G. S., Goldberg, J. R., & Salmon, R. (1971). Supervising in groups as a model for today. *Social Casework, 52,* 154–163.

Getzel, G. S., & Salmon, R. (1985). Group supervision: An organizational approach. *The Clinical Supervisor, 3*(1), 27–43.

Gibelman, M., & Schervish, P. H. (1997). Supervision in social work: Characteristics and trends in a changing environment. *The Clinical Supervisor, 16*(2), 1–15.

Gilbert, T. F. (1974). *Levels and structure of performance analysis.* Morristown, NJ: Praxis Corporation.

Gitterman, A. (1972). Comparison of educational models and their influences on supervision. In F. W. Kaslow et al. (Eds.), *Issues in human services* (pp. 18–38). San Francisco: Jossey-Bass.

Gitterman, A., & Miller, I. (1977). Supervisors as educators. In F. W. Kaslow et al. (Eds.), *Supervision, consultation, staff training in the helping professions* (pp. 100–114). San Francisco: Jossey-Bass.

Glisson, C. A. (1985). A contingency model of social welfare administration. In S. Slavin (Ed.), *An introduction to human services management—Volume I of Social administration: The management of the social services* (pp. 95–109). New York: Haworth Press.

Goodenough, W. H. (1961). Comment on cultural revolution. *Daedalus, 90,* 521–528.

Goodenough, W. H. (1996). Definition. In D. Levinson & M. Ember (Eds.), *Encyclopedia of cultural anthropology* (pp. 291–299). New York: Henry Holt and Company.

Goodman, P. S., & Fichman, M. (1983). Comments on Mitchell. In F. Landy, S. Zedeck, J. Cleveland, & A. Landy (Eds.), *Performance measurement and theory* (pp. 60–74). Hillsdale, NJ: Erlbaum.

Granello, D. H. (1996). Gender and power in the supervisory dyad. *The Clinical Supervisor, 14*(2), 53–67.

Granvold, D. K. (1977). Supervisory style and educational preparation of public welfare supervisors. *Administration in Social Work, 1*(1), 79–88.

Granvold, D. K. (1978a). Supervision by objectives. *Administration in Social Work, 2*(2), 199–209.

Granvold, D. K. (1978b). Training social work supervisors to meet organizational and worker objectives. *Journal of Education for Social Work, 14*(2), 38–45.

Gray, S. W. (1990). The interplay of social work and supervision: An exploratory study. *The Clinical Supervisor, 8*(1), 53–65.

Greenspan, R., Hanfling, S., Parker, E., Primm, S., & Waldfogel, D. (1991). Supervision of experienced agency workers: A descriptive study. *The Clinical Supervisor, 9*(2), 31–42.

Greetz, C. (1973). *The interpretation of cultures: Selected essays.* New York: Basic Books.

Gross, E. (2000). Connected scholarship. *AFFILIA: Journal of Women and Social Work, 15*(1), 5–8.

Guttman, E., Eisikovitz, Z., & Maluccio, A. N. (1988). Enriching social work supervision from the competence perspective. *Journal of Social Work Education, 24*(3), 278–288.

Hardcastle, D. (1991). Towards a model for supervision: A peer supervision pilot project. *The Clinical Supervisor, 9*(2), 63–76.

Harkness, D. (1995). The art of helping in supervised practice: Skills, relationships, and outcomes. *The Clinical Supervisor, 13*(1), 63–76.

Harkness, D. (1997). Testing interactional social work theory: A panel analysis of supervised practice and outcomes. *The Clinical Supervisor, 15*(1), 33–50.

Harkness, D., & Hensley, H. (1991). Changing the focus of social work supervision: Effects on client satisfaction and generalized contentment. *Social Work, 37,* 506–512.

Harkness, D., & Poertner, J. (1989). Research and social work supervision: A conceptual review. *Social Work, 34*(2), 115–118.

Harkness, L., & Mulinski, P. (1988). Performance standards for social workers. *Social Work, 33,* 339–344.

Harris, T. A. (1967). *I'm OK, You're OK.* London: Pan Books.

Hart, G. M. (1982). *The process of clinical supervision.* Baltimore, MD: University Park Press.

Hasenfeld, Y. (1983). *Human service organizations.* Englewood Cliffs, NJ: Prentice-Hall.

Hawkins, P., & Shohet, R. (1990). *Supervision in the helping professions.* London: Open University Press.

Hawthorne, L. (1975). Games supervisors play. *Social Work, 20,* 179–183.

Heid, L. (1997). Supervisor development across the professional lifespan. *The Clinical Supervisor, 16*(2), 139–152.

Heimann, B., & Pittenger, K. S. (1996). The impact of formal mentorship on socialization and commitment of newcomers. *Journal of Managerial Issues, 8*(1), 108–117.

Henderson, R. L. (1984). *Performance appraisal.* Weston, VA: Weston.

Hess, A. K. (1980). *Psychotherapy supervision: Theory, research and practice.* New York: Wiley.

Hess, A. K. (1986). Growth in supervision: Stages of supervisee and supervisor development. *The Clinical Supervisor, 4*(1–2), 51–67.

Hess, A. K. (1987). Psychotherapy supervision: Stages, Buber, and a theory of relationship. *Professional Psychology, 18,* 251–259.

Hester, M. C. (1951). Educational process in supervision. *Social Casework, 25,* 242–250.

Himle, D. P., Jayaratne, S., & Thyness, P. A. (1989). The buffering effects of four types of supervisory support on work stress. *Administration in Social Work, 13*(1), 19–34.

Hipp, J. L., & Munson, C. E. (1995). The partnership model: A feminist supervision/consultation perspective. *The Clinical Supervisor, 13*(1), 23–38.

Holloway, E. (1995). *Clinical supervision: A systems approach.* Newbury Park, CA: Sage.

Holloway, S., & Brager, G. (1989). *Supervising in the human services: The politics of practice.* New York: Free Press.

Howe, E. (1980). Public professions and the private model of professionalism. *Social Work, 25,* 179–191.

Hughes, L., & Pengelly, P. (1997). *Staff supervision in a turbulent environment: Managing process and task in front-line services.* London: Jessica Kingsley.

Ingold, T. (Ed.). (1994). *Companion encyclopedia of anthropology: Humanity, culture and social life.* London: Routledge.

Jenks, C. (1993). *Culture: Key ideas.* London: Routledge.

Johnson, E. W. (1988). Burnout: A metaphoric myth. *American Journal of Physical and Medical Rehabilitation, 67,* 237.

Johnson, T. J. (1972). *Professionals and power.* London: Macmillan.

Kadushin, A. (1968). Games people play in supervision. *Social Work, 13*(3), 23–32.

Kadushin, A. (1974). Supervisor-supervisee: A survey. *Social Work, 19*(3), 288–298.

Kadushin, A. (1976). *Supervision in social work.* New York: Columbia University Press.

Kadushin, A. (1979). Games people play in supervision. In C. E. Munson (Ed.), *Social work supervision: Classic statements and critical issues* (pp. 182–195). New York: Free Press.

Kadushin, A. (1981). Professional development, supervision, training, and education. In N. Gilbert & H. Specht (Eds.), *Handbook of the social services* (pp. 638–665). Englewood Cliffs, NJ: Prentice-Hall.

Kadushin, A. (1985). *Supervision in social work* (2nd ed.). New York: Columbia University Press.

Kadushin, A. (1991). Field education in social work: Contemporary issues and trends. In D. Schneck, B. Grossman, & U. Glassman (Eds.), *Field education in social work* (pp. 11–16). Dubuque, IA: Kendall/Hunt.

Kadushin, A. (1992a). *Supervision in social work* (3rd ed.). New York: Columbia University Press.

Kadushin, A. (1992b). What's wrong, what's right with social work supervision? *The Clinical Supervisor, 10*(1), 3–19.

Kadushin, A. (1992c). Social work supervision: An updated survey. *The Clinical Supervisor, 10*(2), 9–27.

Kadushin, A., & Harkness, D. (2002). *Supervision in social work* (4th ed.). New York: Columbia University Press.

Kahn, E. M. (1979). The parallel process in social work treatment and supervision. *Social Casework, 60,* 520–528.

Kaiser, T. L. (1997). *Supervisory relationships: Exploring the human elements.* Pacific Grove, CA: Brooks/Cole.

Kaplan, T. (1991). A model for group supervision for social work: Implementations for the profession. In D. Schneck, B. Grossman, & U. Glassman (Eds.), *Field education in social work: Contemporary issues and trends* (pp. 141–148). Dubuque, IA: Kendall/Hunt.

Karasek, R., & Theorell, T. (1990). *Healthy work—stress, productivity and the reconstruction of working life.* New York: Basic Books.

Kaslow, F. W. (1972). Group supervision. In F. W. Kaslow et al. (Eds.), *Issues in human services* (pp. 115–141). San Francisco: Jossey-Bass.

Kaslow, F. W. (1986a). Supervision, consultation and staff training—Creative teaching/learning processes in the mental health profession. *The Clinical Supervisor, 4,* 1–28.

Kaslow, F. W. (1986b). Themes and patterns in supervision. In F. W. Kaslow (Ed.), *Supervision and training: Models, dilemmas and challenges* (pp. 237–250). New York: Haworth Press.

Kaslow, F. W., et al. (Eds.). (1977). *Supervision, consultation, and staff training in the helping professions.* San Francisco: Jossey-Bass.

Kaslow, F. W., et al. (1979). *Supervision, consultation, and staff training in the helping professions.* San Francisco: Jossey-Bass.

Kast, F. E., & Rosenzweig, J. E. (1985). *Organization and management: A systems and contingency approach* (4th ed.). New York: McGraw-Hill.

Keesing, R. (1981). *Cultural anthropology: A contemporary perspective* (2nd ed.). New York: Harcourt Brace.

Kelly, M. J. (2001). Management mentoring in a social service organization. *Administration in Social Work, 25*(1), 17–33.

Kennedy, M., & Keitner, L. (1970). What is supervision: The need for a redefinition. *Social Worker, 38,* 51–52.

Kim, Y. O. (1995). Cultural pluralism and Asian-American culturally sensitive social work practice. *International Social Work, 38,* 69–78.

Ko, G. P. (1987). Casework supervision in voluntary family service agencies in Hong Kong. *International Social Work, 30,* 171–184.

Koontz, H. (1961). The management theory jungle. *Academy of Management Journal, 4,* 174–188.

Koontz, H. (1980). The management theory jungle revisited. *Academy of Management Review, 5*, 175–187.

Kroeber, A. L., & Kluckhohn, C. (1952). *Culture: A critical review of concepts and definitions*. Cambridge, MA: Peabody Museum.

Kutzik, A. J. (1977). The social work field. In F. W. Kaslow et al. (Eds.), *Supervision, consultation, and staff training in the helping professions* (pp. 25–60). San Francisco: Jossey-Bass.

Lahad, M. (2000). *Creative supervision: The use of expressive arts methods in supervision and self-supervision*. London: Jessica Kingsley.

Landy, F. L., & Farr, J. L. (1990). Performance rating. *Psychology Bulletin, 87*(1), 72–107.

Latting, J. E. (1986). Adaptive supervision: A theoretical model for social workers. *Administration in Social Work, 10*(1), 15–23.

Lee, M. Y. (1996). A constructivist approach to the help-seeking process of clients: A response to cultural diversity. *Clinical Social Work Journal, 24*(2), 187–202.

Leiren, B. D. (1990). *Workplace performance evaluation*. Vancouver, BC: Eduserv Inc.

LeVine, R. A. (1984). Properties of culture: An ethnographic view. In R. A. Shweder & R. A. LeVine (Eds.), *Culture theory: Essays on mind, self, and emotion* (pp. 67–87). Cambridge, UK: Cambridge University Press.

Levy, C. S. (1973, March). The ethics of supervision. *Social Work*, 14–21.

Lewis, S. (1988). The role of self-awareness in social work supervision. *Australian Social Work, 40*(2), 19–24.

Lewis, W. (1988). A supervision model for public agencies. *The Clinical Supervisor, 6*(2), 85–91.

Liddle, H., & Saba, G. (1983). On context replication: The isomorphic relationship of training and therapy. *The Journal of Strategic and Systematic Therapies, 2*, 3–11.

Lipsky, M. (1980). *Street-level bureaucracy: Dilemmas of the individual in public services*. New York: Russell Sage Foundation.

Loganbill, C., Hardy, E., & Delworth, U. (1982). Supervision: A conceptual model. *The Counseling Psychologist, 10*(1), 3–42.

Lowy, L. (1983). Social work supervision: From models toward theory. *Journal of Education for Social Work, 19*(2), 55–62.

MacIver, R. M. (1965). *The web of government* (Rev. ed.). New York: Macmillan.

Mandell, B. (1973). The "equality" revolution and supervision. *Journal of Education for Social Work, 9*, 43–54.

McKitrick, D. S., & Garrison, M. A. (1992). Theory of supervision outline: A training tool. *The Clinical Supervisor, 19*(2), 173–183.

Melichercik, J. (1984). Social work supervision in transition: An exploration of current supervisory practice. *The Social Worker, 52*(3), 108–112.

Middleman, R. R., & Rhodes, G. B. (1980). Teaching the practice of supervision. *Journal of Education for Social Work, 16*(3), 51–59.

Middleman, R. R., & Rhodes, G. B. (1985). *Competent supervision: Making imaginative judgements.* Englewood Cliffs, NJ: Prentice-Hall.

Miller, I. (1987). Supervision in social work. In *Encyclopedia of social work* (Vol. 2, pp. 748–756). Silver Spring, MD: National Association of Social Workers.

Morgan, S., & Payne, M. (2002). Managerialism and state social work. *Hong Kong Journal of Social Work, 36*(1), 27–44.

Munson, C. E. (1975). *The uses of structural, authority and teaching models in social work supervision.* Unpublished doctoral dissertation, University of Maryland.

Munson, C. E. (1976). Professional autonomy and social work supervision. *Journal of Education for Social Work, 12*(3), 95–102.

Munson, C. E. (1978a). The concepts of effectiveness and efficiency applied to the social work profession: An historical perspective. *Journal of Education for Social Work, 14*(2), 90–97.

Munson, C. E. (1978b). The worker/client relationship: Relevant role theory. *Journal of Sociology and Social Welfare, 5*(3), 404–417.

Munson, C. E. (1979a). Authority and social work supervision: An emerging model. In C. E. Munson (Ed.), *Social work supervision: Classic statements and critical issues* (pp. 336–346). New York: Free Press.

Munson, C. E. (1979b). An empirical study of structure and authority in social work supervision. In C. E. Munson (Ed.), *Social work supervision: Classic statements and critical issues* (pp. 286–296). New York: Free Press.

Munson, C. E. (1979c). Evaluation of male and female supervisors. *Social Work, 24,* 104–110.

Munson, C. E. (Ed.). (1979d). *Social work supervision: Classic statements and critical issues.* New York: Free Press.

Munson, C. E. (1979e). Symbolic interaction and social work supervision. *Journal of Sociology and Social Welfare, 6*(1), 8–18.

Munson, C. E. (1981). Style and structure in supervision. *Journal of Education for Social Work, 17*(1), 65–72.

Munson, C. E. (1983). *An introduction to clinical social work supervision.* New York: Haworth Press.

Munson, C. E. (1987a). Sex roles and power relationships in supervision. *Professional Psychology: Research and Practice, 18*(3), 236–243.

Munson, C. E. (1987b). Field instruction in social work education. *Journal of Teaching in Social Work, 1*(1), 91–109.

Munson, C. E. (1989). Trends of significance for clinical supervision. *The Clinical Supervisor, 7*(4), 1–8.

Munson, C. E. (1993). *Clinical social work supervision* (2nd ed.). New York: Haworth Press.

Munson, C. E. (1998). Societal change, managed cost organizations, and clinical social work practice. *The Clinical Supervisor, 17*(2), 1–41.

Munson, C. E. (2002). *Handbook of clinical social work supervision* (3rd ed.). New York: Haworth Press.

Newsome, M., Jr., & Pillari, V. (1991). Job satisfaction and the worker-supervisor relationship. *The Clinical Supervisor, 9*(2), 119–129.

Nichols, F. W. (1977). Concerning performance and performance standards: An opinion. *NSPI Journal, 16*(1), 14–17.

O'Donoghue, K. (2003). *Restorying social work supervision.* Palmerston North, New Zealand: Dunmore Press.

Olsen, D. C., & Stern, S. B. (1990). Issues in the development of a family supervision model. *The Clinical Supervisor, 8*(2), 49–65.

Orchard, B. (1971). The use of authority in supervision. In S. A. Yelaja (Ed.), *Authority and social work: Concept and use* (pp. 278–288). Toronto: University of Toronto Press.

Osborne, C. J., & Davis, T. E. (1996). The supervision contract: Making it perfectly clear. *The Clinical Supervisor, 14*(2), 121–134.

Osborne, S. P. (1992). The quality dimension: Evaluating quality of service and quality of life in human services. *British Journal of Social Work, 22,* 437–453.

Osterberg, M. J. (1996). Gender in supervision: Exaggerating the differences between men and women. *The Clinical Supervisor, 14*(2), 69–84.

Palmer, S. (1983, March–April). Authority: An essential part of practice. *Social Work,* 120–125.

Parsloe, P., & Stevenson, O. (1978). *Social service teams: The practitioner's view.* London: Her Majesty's Stationery Office.

Parsons, J. E., & Durst, D. (1992). Learning contracts: Misunderstood and utilized. *The Clinical Supervisor, 10*(1), 145–156.

Parton, N. (2003). Rethinking professional practice: The contribution of social constructionism and the feminist "ethics of care." *The British Journal of Social Work, 33*(1), 1–16.

Patti, R. J. (1985). In search of purpose for social welfare administration. *Administration in Social Work, 9*(3), 1–14.

Patti, R. J. (1988). Managing for service effectiveness in social welfare: Towards a performance model. In R. J. Patti, J. Poertner, & C. A. Rapp (Eds.), *Managing for service effectiveness in social welfare organizations* (pp. 7–22). New York: Haworth Press.

Patti, R. J., Poertner, J., & Rapp, C. A. (Eds.). (1988). *Managing for service effectiveness in social welfare organizations.* New York: Haworth Press.

Payne, C., & Scott, T. (1982). *Developing supervision of teams in field and residential social work.* London: National Institute for Social Work.

Payne, M. (1979). *Power, authority and responsibility in social services.* London: Macmillan Press.

Payne, M. (1994). Personal supervision in social work. In A. Connor & S. Black (Eds.), *Performance review and quality in social care* (pp. 43–58). London: Jessica Kingsley.

Perlmutter, F. D. (1990). *Changing hats: From social work practice to administration.* Silver Spring, MD: National Association of Social Workers.

Perlmutter, F. D., Bailey, D., & Netting, F. E. (2001). *Managing human resources in the human services: Supervisory challenges.* Oxford: Oxford University Press.

Peterson, F. K. (1991). Issues of race and ethnicity in supervision: Emphasizing who you are, not what you know. *The Clinical Supervisor, 9,* 15–31.

Pettes, D. (1967). *Supervision in social work: A method of student training and staff development.* London: Allen & Unwin.

Pettes, D. E. (1979). *Staff and student supervision: A task-centered approach.* London: Allen & Unwin.

Pilcher, A. J. (1984). The state of social work supervision in Victoria according to the practitioners. *Australian Social Work, 37*(3/4), 33–43.

Poertner, J. (1986). The use of client feedback to improve practice: Defining the supervisor's role. *The Clinical Supervisor, 4*(4), 57–67.

Poertner, J., & Rapp, C. A. (1983). What is social work supervision? *The Clinical Supervisor, 1*(2), 53–67.

Pollitt, C. (1993). *Managerialism and the public service* (2nd ed.). Oxford: Blackwell.

Poulin, J. E. (1995). Job satisfaction of social work supervisors and administrators. *Administration in Social Work, 19*(4), 35–49.

Powell, D. J. (1980). *Clinical supervision: Skills for substance counselors.* New York: Human Science Press.

Powell, D. J. (1993). *Clinical supervision in alcohol and drug abuse counseling: Principles, models, methods.* New York: Lexington Books.

Powell, G. (1994). One more time: Do female and male managers differ? In M. F. Karsten (Ed.), *Management and gender: Issues and attitudes* (pp. 87–93). Westport, CT: Praeger.

Pritchard, J. (Ed.). (1995). *Good practice in supervision: Statutory and voluntary organizations.* London: Jessica Kingsley.

Quick, J. C., & Quick, J. D. (1984). *Organizational stress and preventive management.* New York: McGraw-Hill.

Quinn, J. B., Anderson, P., & Finkelstein, S. (1998). Management professional intellect: Making the most of the best. Cambridge, MA: Harvard Business School Press.

Rabinowitz, J. (1987). Why ongoing supervision in social casework: An historical analysis. *The Clinical Supervisor, 5*(3), 79–90.

Ragins, B. R., & Scandura, T. A. (1994). Gender differences in expected outcomes of mentoring relationships. *Academy of Management Journal, 37,* 957–971.

Rauktis, M. E., & Koeske, G. F. (1994). Maintaining social worker morale: When supportive supervision is not enough. *Administration in Social Work, 18*(1), 39–60.

Reid, W. J. (1988). Service effectiveness and the social agency. In R. J. Patti, J. Poertner, & C. A. Rapp (Eds.), *Managing for service effectiveness in social welfare organizations* (pp. 41–58). New York: Haworth Press.

Rich, P. (1993). The form, function, and content of clinical supervision: An integrated model. *The Clinical Supervisor, 11*(1), 137–178.

Richmond, M. (1917). *Social diagnosis.* New York: Russell Sage Foundation.

Ritchie, P. (1992). Establishing standards in social care. In D. Kelly & B. Warr (Eds.), *Quality counts: Achieving quality in social care services* (pp. 57–75). London: Whiting & Birch.

Rivas, R. F. (1991). Dismissing problem employees. In R. L. Edwards & J. A. Yankey (Eds.), *Skills for effective human services management* (pp. 186–216). Silver Spring, MD: National Association of Social Workers.

Robinson, V. (1936). *Supervision in social case work.* Chapel Hill, NC: University of North Carolina Press.

Robinson, V. (1949). *The dynamics of supervision under functional controls.* Philadelphia: University of Pennsylvania Press.

Rock, B. (1990). Social worker autonomy in the age of accountability. *The Clinical Supervisor, 8*(2), 19–31.

Rogers, E. R. (1987). Professional burnout: A review of a concept. *The Clinical Supervisor, 5*(3), 91–106.

Rogers, G., & McDonald, L. (1992). Thinking critically: An approach to field instructor training. *Journal of Social Work Education, 28*(2), 166–177.

Rubin, A., & Babbie, E. R. (1997). *Research methods for social work.* Pacific Grove, CA: Brooks/Cole.

Rubinstein, G. (1992). Supervision and psychotherapy: Toward redefining the differences. *The Clinical Supervisor, 10*(2), 97–116.

Russell, R. K., Crinnings, A. M., & Lent, R. W. (1984). Counselor training and supervision: Theory and research. In S. D. Brown & R. W. Lent (Eds.), *Handbook of counseling psychology* (pp. 625–681). New York: Wiley.

Russell, P. A., Lankford, M. W., & Grinnell, R. M. (1983). Attitudes toward supervisors in a human service agency. *The Clinical Supervisor, 1*(3), 57–71.

Sales, E., & Navarre, E. (1970). *Individual and group supervision in field instruction: A research report.* Ann Arbor, MI: School of Social Work, University of Michigan.

Sarri, C. (1986). Concepts of learning through supervision. *The Clinical Supervisor, 4*(3), 63–78.

Schindler, N. J., & Talen, M. R. (1996). Supervision 101: The basic elements for teaching beginning supervisors. *The Clinical Supervisor, 14*(2), 109–120.

Schneier, C. E., & Beatty, R. W. (1982). What is performance appraisal? In L. Baird et al. (Eds.), *The performance appraisal sourcebook.* Amherst, MA: Human Resource Development Press.

Schour, E. (1951). Helping social workers to handle work stress. *Social Casework, 25,* 423–438.

Schreiber, P., & Frank, E. (1983). The use of a peer supervision group by social work clinicians. *The Clinical Supervisor, 1*(1), 29–36.

Scott, D., & Farrow, J. (1993). Evaluating standards of social work supervision in child welfare and hospital social work. *Australian Social Work, 46*(2), 33–41.

Scott, W. R. (1965). Reactions to supervision in a heteronomous professional organization. *Administrative Science Quarterly, 10,* 65–81.

Scott, W. R. (1979). Reactions to supervision in a heteronomous professional organization. In C. E. Munson (Ed.), *Social work supervision: Classic statements and critical issues* (pp. 258–272). New York: Free Press.

Segall, M. H. (1984). More than we need to know about culture, but are afraid not to ask. *Journal of Cross-Cultural Psychology, 15*(2), 153–162.

Sennett, R. (1980). *Authority.* New York: Knopf.

Sergiovanni, T. J. (1983). *Supervision: A perspective* (3rd ed.). New York: McGraw-Hill.

Shinn, M., Rosario, M., Morch, H., & Chestnut, D. E. (1984). Coping with job stress and burnout in the human services. *Journal of Personality and Social Psychology, 40,* 864–976.

Shulman, L. (1993). *Interactional supervision.* Washington, DC: NASW Press.

Shulman, L. (1995). Supervision and consultation. In *Encyclopedia of Social Work* (pp. 2373–2379). Silver Spring, MD: National Association of Social Workers.

Shulman, L., Robinson, E., & Luckj, A. (1981). *A study of the content, context and skills of supervision.* Vancouver: University of British Columbia.

Skidmore, R. A. (1995). *Social work administration: Dynamic management and human relationships* (3rd ed.). Boston: Allyn & Bacon.

Soderfeldt, M., Soderfeldt, B., & Warg, L. (1995). Burnout in social work. *Social Work, 40*(5), 638–646.

Specht, H., & Courtney, M. (1994). *Unfaithful angels: How social work has abandoned its mission.* New York: Free Press.

Stevens, D. T., Goodyear, R. K., & Robertson, P. (1997). Supervisor development: An exploratory study in changes in stances and emphasis. *The Clinical Supervisor, 16*(2), 73–88.

Stiles, E. (1979). Supervision in perspective. In C. E. Munson (Ed.), *Social work supervision: Classical statements and critical issues* (pp. 83–93). New York: Free Press.

Stoltenberg, C. (1981). Approaching supervision from a developmental perspective: The counselor complexity model. *Journal of Counseling Psychology, 28*(1), 59–65.

Stoltenberg, C. D., & Delworth, U. (1987). *Supervising counselor and therapists: A developmental approach.* San Francisco: Jossey-Bass.

Storm, C. L., & Heath, A. W. (1985). Models of supervision: Using therapy theory as a guide. *The Clinical Supervisor, 3*(1), 87–96.

Thompson, N., Stradling, S., Murphy, M., & O'Neill, P. (1996). Stress and organizational culture. *British Journal of Social Work, 26,* 647–665.

Towle, C. (1954). *The learner in education for the professions.* Chicago: University of Chicago Press.

Towle, C. (1962). The role of supervision in the union of cause and function in social work. *Social Service Review, 36,* 396–411.

Tsang, A. K. T., & George, U. (1998). Towards an integrated framework for cross-cultural social work practice. *Canadian Social Work Review, 15*(1), 73–93.

Tsui, M. S. (1997a). The roots of social work supervision: An historical review. *The Clinical Supervisor, 15*(2), 191–198.

Tsui, M. S. (1997b). Empirical research on social work supervision: The state of the art (1970–1995). *Journal of Social Service Research, 23*(2), 39–54.

Tsui, M. S. (1998a). Construction of a job performance model for professional social workers. *Asia Pacific Journal of Social Work, 8*(2), 51–63.

Tsui, M. S. (1998b). Organizations as elephants: A Chinese metaphor or a metatheory? *International Journal of Management, 15*(2), 151–160.

Tsui, M. S. (2001). *Towards a culturally sensitive model of social work supervision in Hong Kong.* Unpublished doctoral dissertation, Faculty of Social Work, University of Toronto.

Tsui, M. S. (2002). Social work supervision in Hong Kong: An exploration of objectives, structure, and relationship. In D. Shek (Ed.), *Entering a new millennium: Advances in social welfare in Hong Kong* (pp. 253–269) (in Chinese). Hong Kong: Chinese University Press.

Tsui, M. S. (2004). Charting the course of future research on supervision. In M. J. Austin & K. M. Hopkins (Eds.), *Supervising in the human services: Building a learning organization.* Thousand Oaks, CA: Sage.

Tsui, M. S. (in press). Functions of social work supervision in Hong Kong. *International Social Work.*

Tsui, M. S., & Chan, R. K. H. (1999). The future of social work: A revision and a vision. *Indian Journal of Social Work, 60*(1), 87–98.

Tsui, M. S., & Cheung, F. C. H. (2000a). Reflection over social welfare administration (in Chinese). *Hong Kong Journal of Social Work, 34*(1&2), 91–101.

Tsui, M. S., & Cheung, F. C. H. (2000b). Nature of social work administration. In C. K. Ho (Ed.), *Paradigms and nature: Reflections on social work* (in Chinese). Singapore: World Scientific.

Tsui, M. S., & Cheung, F. C. H. (2004). Gone with the wind: The impacts of managerialism on human services. *The British Journal of Social Work, 34,* 437–442.

Tsui, M. S., Cheung, F. C. H., & Gellis, Z. D. (2004). In search of an optimal model for board-executive relationships in voluntary human service organizations. *International Social Work, 47*(2), 169–186.

Tsui, M. S., & Ho, W. S. (1997). In search of a comprehensive model of social work supervision. *The Clinical Supervisor, 16*(2), 181–205.

Tsui, M. S., & Ho, W. S. (2003). *Social work supervision: Theory, practice, and reflection* (in Chinese). Hong Kong: Hong Kong Christian Service.

Tylor, E. B. (1871). *Primitive culture.* London: Murray.

Vayda, E., & Bogo, M. (1991). A teaching model to unite classroom and field. *Journal of Social Work Education, 27*(3), 271–278.

Veeder, N. W. (1990). Autonomy, accountability, and professionalism: The case against close supervision in social work. *The Clinical Supervisor, 8*(2), 33–47.

Vinokur-Kaplan, D. (1987). A national survey of in-service training experiences of child welfare supervisors and workers. *Social Service Review, 61*(2), 291–304.

Waldfogel, D. (1983). Supervision of students and practitioners. In A. Rosenblatt & D. Waldfogel (Eds.), *Handbook of clinical social work* (pp. 319–344). San Francisco: Jossey-Bass.

Wallace, J. E., & Brinkerhoff, M. B. (1991). The measurement of burnout revisited. *Journal of Social Service Research, 14*(1/2), 85–111.

Watkins, C. E., Jr. (1990). Development of the psychotherapy supervisor. *Psychotherapy, 27*(4), 553–560.

Watkins, C. E., Jr. (1993). Development of the psychotherapy supervisor: Concepts, assumptions, and hypotheses of the supervisor complexity model. *American Journal of Psychotherapy, 47*(1), 58–74.

Watson, K. W. (1973). Differential supervision. *Social Work, 8*(3), 37–43.

Wax, J. (1979). The pros and cons of group supervision. *Social Casework, 40*(56), 307–313.

Weinbach, R. W. (1992). Meeting a supervisory responsibility: Shared evaluation of supervisory potential. *The Clinical Supervisor, 10*(2), 195–209.

Western New York Chapter, NASW Committee on Social Work. (1958). A chapter survey. *Social Work, 3*, 18–25.

Westheimer, I. J. (1977). *The practice of supervision in social work: A guide for staff supervisors.* London: Ward Lock Educational.

White, M. B., & Russell, C. S. (1995). The essential elements of supervisory systems: A modified delphi study. *Journal of Marital and Family Therapy, 21*(1), 33–53.

Williams, A. J. (1988). Action methods in supervision. *The Clinical Supervisor, 6*(2), 13–27.

Wilson, S. A. (1981). *Field instruction: Techniques for supervisors.* New York: Free Press.

Worthington, E. L., Jr. (1984). Empirical investigation of supervision of counselors as they can experience. *Journal of Counseling Psychology, 31*(1), 63–75.

Yan, M. C., & Tsui, M. S. (2003). *Flipping focus for survival: The culture of the social work profession.* Unpublished manuscript.

York, R. O., & Denton, R. T. (1990). Leadership behavior and supervisory performance: The view from below. *The Clinical Supervisor, 8*(1), 93–108.

York, R. O., & Hastings, T. (1985). Worker maturity and supervisory leadership behavior. *Administration in Social Work, 9*(4), 37–46.

Index

About the Author

Ming-sum Tsui is Senior Lecturer in Social Work, Department of Applied Social Sciences, Hong Kong Polytechnic University, where he teaches social work supervision and human service management. Ming-sum has more than 20 years of experience in practicing and teaching social work supervision. Before joining the Hong Kong Polytechnic University, he was service supervisor of development and health services at the second largest voluntary social welfare agency in Hong Kong, the Hong Kong Christian Service. More than two decades ago, Ming-sum started his social work career in a community-based children and youth center. In his 10 years of service in the Hong Kong Christian Service, he set up the first community-based family service center and the first counseling center for psychotropic substance abusers in Hong Kong. He also supervised a polyclinic and was responsible for program development, fund raising, research, program evaluation, and staff development of the Hong Kong Christian Service.

Ming-sum received his undergraduate social work education at the Chinese University of Hong Kong, and later received an MSW from McGill University and a Postgraduate Diploma in Management Studies from the Hong Kong Polytechnic University. He is a member of the Academy of Certified Social Workers (ACSW) and was the first international member of Certified Social Work Managers (CSWM). He is also a member of the American Management Association (AMA), Chartered Management Institute (CMI), and a Certified ISO Auditor. Ming-sum earned his Ph.D. in the Faculty of Social Work at the University of Toronto. His thesis research is on the construction of a culturally sensitive model of social work supervision.

The research interests of Ming-sum are related to social work supervision, human service management, the theory and practice of social work, and substance abuse. He has been the managing editor of the *Hong Kong Journal of Social Work*, consulting editor of *New Global*

Development, Families-in-Society, and member of the editorial board of *Research on Social Work Practice, Employee Assistance Quarterly,* and *Professional Development: International Journal of Continuing Social Work Education.* He also serves as an expert reviewer for 15 journals. Mingsum has published 10 books and more than 70 articles and research papers. His work has been widely published in academic and professional journals all over the world, including *Journal of Social Service Research, The Clinical Supervisor, Social Work, Families in Society, International Social Work, International Journal of Management, New Global Development: International Journal of Comparative Social Welfare, The British Journal of Social Work, Social Development Issues, Asia Pacific Journal of Social Work, Hong Kong Journal of Social Work, Asian Journal of Counseling, Australian Social Work, China Social Work, Indian Journal of Social Work, Assessment & Research in Higher Education, Employee Assistance Quarterly,* and *Child and Adolescent Social Work Journal.*

Printed in the United Kingdom
by Lightning Source UK Ltd.
127065UK00001B/43-45/A